Video Engineering Fundamentals:
A Digital Troublemaker Guide

By Pierre (Pete) Routhier
Copyright © 2024 by Creat3 inc.

All rights reserved. No part of this book may be reproduced or transmitted in any form or by any means without written permission from the author.

Cover Art by Justine Routhier © 2024 by Creat3 inc.
All Rights Reserved

The Digital Troublemaker Guides

Our guides for digital production and post-production are based on three simple principles:

1. **NEUTRALITY**. We strive to provide the most objective view of the different technologies, processes, and workflows that we cover in our guides. Data and information we gather during our research and in our lab is validated as much as possible with independent, third-party sources. We do not advertise, nor do we get donations from anyone selling products or services that we cover.

2. **THOROUGHNESS**. When we deal with a subject, we aim to cover as much ground as there is to cover. So, when you're done with this guide, you should have a wide understanding of the issues, the key players, the opportunities, and the challenges.

3. **ACCESSIBILITY**. You don't have to be a technical expert to read this guide. We do our very best to provide clear, easy to understand examples and graphics, and avoid complex equations and formulas so anyone can acquire key knowledge.

Table of Contents

The Digital Troublemaker Guides	2
Table of Contents	3
Your first days in this industry…	8
1. File-based video	9
1.1 Spatial Resolution	10
1.1.1 Aspect Ratio	12
1.2 Temporal Resolution	12
1.2.1 Fields vs. Frames	14
1.2.2 Progressive versus psf	16
1.2.3 3:2 pulldown	17
1.2.4 High Frame Rate (HFR)	18
1.2.5 Frame Rate summary	18
1.3 Bit Depth	19
1.3.1 Banding	20
1.4 Luminance and Color Resolution	22
1.4.1 How our eyes perceive luminance and color	22
1.4.2 How digital cameras perceive light	26
1.4.3 Color representation in Video production	28
1.4.4 Color Spaces in Video for Television and Cinema	29
1.4.5 Chroma sub-sampling	31
1.4.6 Transfer Functions: EOTF, OETF, OOTF	32
1.4.6.1 Hybrid Log-Gamma (HLG) Transfer Function	35
1.4.6.2 Perceptual Quantizer (PQ) Transfer Function	35

      1.4.6.3 Vendor-Specific Transfer Functions (VLog, SLog, LogC, CLog, etc.)   36

      1.4.6.4 Scene linear, scene-referred, and display-referred   37

  1.5 Putting it all together   38

2. Video Compression and Decompression   40

  2.1 Lossless codecs   41

  2.2 Lossy codecs   41

    2.2.1 I, P and B frames   43

    2.2.2 Codec trade-offs   45

  2.3 Packaging - Video Containers   47

  2.4 Putting it all together   48

    2.4.1 Encoding and packaging with Adobe Media Encoder™   48

    2.4.2 Encoding and packaging with HandBrake   49

    2.4.3 Encoding and packaging with DaVinci Resolve™   51

    2.4.4 Validating the package   51

  2.5 Source, Mezzanine and Distribution formats   54

    2.5.1 Source Assets   54

    2.5.2 Mezzanine   55

    2.5.3 Distribution   55

  2.6 Common Industry Bitrates and Formats   56

    2.6.1 Mpeg-2   56

    2.6.2 H.264   56

    2.6.3 Social Media   56

3. Live video transmission   57

  3.1 Deterministic Video   57

  3.2 Probabilistic workflows   60

    3.2.1 Packets   61

      3.2.1.1 Packet timing   62

    3.2.1.2 Error Prevention and Correction   64
  3.2.2 Packet-based Video-over-IP protocols   65
  3.2.3 Which protocol is right for the job?   66

4. Image Capture Fundamentals   68
  4.1 Cinematography - what goes into an image   68
  4.2 Lighting and its effect on image capture   69
  4.3 Color integrity   70
  4.4 Focus and Depth of Field   73
  4.5 Focal Length and Perspective   74
  4.6 Detail in Video   75
  4.7 Framing and Motion   76
  4.8 The role of image technicians and engineers with regards to Image Capture   77

5. Video Quality Control   78
  5.1 Spatial resolution issues   78
    5.1.1 Out of focus   78
    5.1.2 Aliasing   79
  5.2 Temporal resolution issues   79
    5.2.1 Judder   79
    5.2.2 Excessive motion blur   80
  5.3 Color and light resolution issues   80
    5.3.1 Out of gamut   80
    5.3.2 Clipping   80
    5.3.3 Dark noise   81
    5.3.4 Skin tones and color rendition   81
    5.3.5 Color temperature   81
    5.3.6 Light and Color QC tools   81
      5.3.6.1 Waveform Monitor   82

5.3.6.2 Vectorscope	84
5.3.6.3 Histogram	85
5.3.6.4 False Color (also called Heat Map)	85
5.4 Compression issues	86
5.4.1 Banding	87
5.4.2 Macro blocks	87
5.4.3 Corrupted frames	88
5.5 Automatic quality control software	88
5.6 To learn more	88
6. Graphics Fundamentals	89
6.1 Vector Graphics	89
6.1.1 HTML5 Vector graphic formats	89
6.1.2 Overlaying vector-based graphics on video	90
6.2 Raster Graphics	91
6.2.1 Video transparency - raster graphics	92
6.2.1.1 Keying	93
6.2.1.2 Alpha Matting	93
6.2.2 Raster graphic formats	95
6.3 Compositing graphics - software	95
7. Display Fundamentals	97
7.1 CRT	97
7.2 LCD	98
7.3 QLED LCD	99
7.4 OLED	100
7.4.1 RGB OLED	101
7.4.2 White OLED	102
7.4.3 QD-OLED	103

7.5 MicroLED 104
7.6 Typical uses - different display technologies 106
IN CONCLUSION 108
GLOSSARY 109

Your first days in this industry…

You will likely feel overwhelmed by all the acronyms and specific terms lobbed at you. Speaking for myself I have, more than once, felt insecure and incompetent not understanding what people were talking about.

Even though this book doesn't have the words "Don't Panic!" in big, friendly letters on the cover, you should feel a lot more comfortable with the industry jargon once you've been through it. If you don't feel like reading it from end to end, there's also a rather comprehensive glossary at the end, where many of the "buzzwords" you will hear are defined and explained in plain English.

Outside of this first objective (understanding the industry's rather opaque jargon), the guide should also help you answer the following:

What's the difference between a 300$ action camera and a 100 000$ broadcast camera? Why would you need the latter if the cheaper one captures at the same resolution?

Which workflows should you be using when capturing video files? What about covering a live event?

What do "creatives" like *Directors of Photography* (DP, or DoP), mean when they are talking about their "creative intent"? What choices are they making, and how do those choices affect the image?

Happy reading, and welcome to our fascinating industry!

1. File-based video

File-based video became prevalent after March 2011, one of the main contributing factors being the Tsunami that ravaged Japan, including the main Sony factory where the popular HDCam SR tape-based media was manufactured[1]. Since its inception, the broadcast industry had relied on magnetic tape to record and play back video assets, originally in the form of analog signals then later using digital formats. Now that it was facing a significant shortage, replacement solutions were needed, and quickly.

Around that time, solid-state flash memory was becoming prevalent as an affordable, more robust alternative to tape in the computer industry. Instead of "laying" the video in a linear fashion on feet of tape, the video assets could now be encoded as files, which could be read by a media player on a computer, without requiring any expensive, dedicated playback devices. We may take this for granted today, but it was truly revolutionary at the time, and combined with a lack of tape supply, completely transformed the industry.

We can therefore define modern file-based video as:

A computer file that contains a sequence of images, synchronized sound and additional information called metadata about the file's origin, time of capture, contents, format, and capture settings

---

[1] Giardina, Carolyn. *Industry Scrambling After Japan Earthquake, Tsunami Lead to Tape Shortage.* The Hollywood Reporter, March 20, 2011. Link: https://www.hollywoodreporter.com/business/digital/industry-scrambling-japan-earthquake-tsunami-169456/

It is not unusual for the uninitiated to consider the number of pixels in an image as the ultimate measure of video quality. After all, an *Ultra HD* image, which contains four times more pixels than a *High-Definition* image, should be much clearer, sharper, and overall better, right? This is not necessarily the case. There are a lot of other factors that dictate the quality of an image, and this is what we're now going to look at, namely:

- Spatial Resolution
- Temporal Resolution
- Bit Depth
- Color Gamut
- Color Sub-sampling
- Transfer Function
- Codec
- Container

1.1 Spatial Resolution

Spatial resolution is, as we've mentioned, the first thing that comes to mind to the amateur when thinking about image quality. The number of horizontal and vertical *pixels* making up an image constitute its spatial resolution. In the photo industry, resolution is expressed in *Megapixels*, or millions of pixels, which can be calculated by multiplying the horizontal number of pixels by the vertical number. For example, an image that measures 2000 pixels across by 1000 pixels high has a spatial resolution of 2000 x 1000, or 2 million pixels, hence 2 megapixels.

In the video industry, spatial resolution is rarely expressed that way. Due to broadcast's heritage, where the number of vertical scan lines was originally dictated in analog television systems, the spatial resolution is still expressed, to this day, as a number of lines.

The most common resolutions in broadcast and cinema are as follows:

Standard Definition Television - N. America: 720x480 pixels, or 480i[2]
Standard Definition Television - Other regions: 720 x 576 or 576i
High-Definition Television: 1280 x 720, or 720p
Full High-Definition Television: 1920 x 1080, or 1080i
Digital Cinema: 2048 x 1080, or 2K
Ultra-High Definition: 3840 x 2160, or 2160p
4K Cinema: 4096 x 2160, or 4K
Super Hi Vision: 8192 x 4320, or 4320p

To give you an idea of how far we have come since the first HD broadcast on consumer TVs, in 1998, here is a representation of those resolutions at scale (fig. 1):

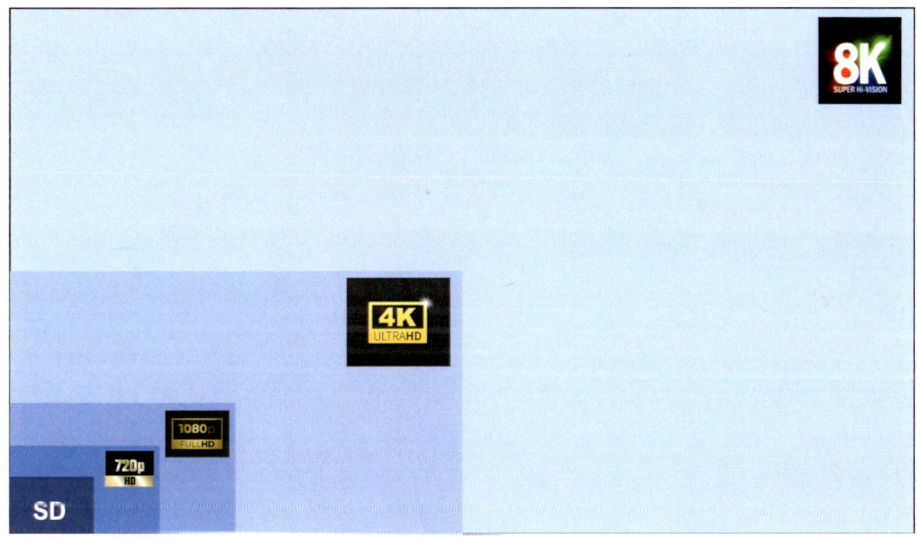

Figure 1 - Spatial Resolutions in Broadcast

The cinema industry, which had a legacy of film, not scan lines on a *Cathode-Ray Tube* (CRT for short), does not express its resolution in the same way, preferring the monikers *2K* and *4K*, which are often incorrectly re-applied back to the television world (as the marketing logos in figure 1 show).

---

[2] We will explain the "i" and "p" notations later in this chapter; don't worry about it for now :)

1.1.1 Aspect Ratio

The *Aspect Ratio* (AR for short) of an image is the ratio of its width in pixels to its height. It can be expressed either as a unitary ratio (e.g. 1.67:1), or as the lowest common denominator values (e.g. 16:9).

In broadcast, aspect ratios are fixed, at 4:3 (or 1.33:1) for Standard Definition and 16:9 (or 1.67:1) for High Definition and above. Cinema is somewhat more complicated; the 2K and 4K resolutions mentioned above are for the image *container*, not the image per se. Within the 2K 2048 x 1080 container, there are two possible ARs: flat at 1.85:1 (or 1998 x 1080), or scope, at 2.39:1 (or 2048 x 858). As you can see, neither uses the whole container. One maxes out the height of the image while the other one maximizes its width. During projection, curtains obscure the black portions of the image, so the empty parts of the container are not visible to the viewer.

On television, tablets and phones, there are no curtains, obviously. So, there are different strategies to cover the fact that sometimes, the full image is not filling the entire screen.

When the image takes the full height, but not the full width, the occlusion on each side of the image is called *pillarbox*. Basically, pillars on each side of the image. The most frequent occurrence of pillarbox is when a 4:3 classic standard definition television image is presented in a 16:9 high-definition frame.

Inversely, when the image takes the full width but not the full height, it is called *letterbox*. The most frequent occurrence of letterbox nowadays is when a wide screen movie (2.39:1) is presented in high definition (16:9).

1.2 Temporal Resolution

What differentiates video from still images is, of course, that images in video are presented to the human eye in rapid succession, giving the viewer the illusion of motion. In the pioneering years of cinema, the number of images per second would vary as both capture and playback were done manually. Some went as far as to use speed as a storytelling device, giving detailed instructions to projectionists on how fast or slow they should crank the projector depending on the scene. Theater owners would sometimes ask their projectionists to play movies faster than the originating studio specified, to squeeze more projections in the day hence increase revenue. All this changed in the 1920s, with the introduction of motorized projection and, eventually, synchronized sound being added to the image.

For cinema, multiple frame rates were used, until the industry settled, more or less arbitrarily, on the current standard of 24 frames per second, which was some sort of compromise between heavy flickering (which occurs when the frame rate is too low) and the cost of film.

For television, which relied on electrical power to operate, frame rates were dictated by the current standard in the country of operation. Hence, North American countries like the United States and Canada, whose power was cycled at 60Hz (or 60 cycles per second), adopted 60 fields per second, whereas African, Oceanian, European and Asian countries whose power is cycled at 50Hz used 50 fields per second.

Now, you may have heard that North America uses 59.94 and not 60 as a video frequency (frames per second). This is true. When black-and-white television shifted to color, The National Television System Committee (NTSC) shifted video frequency slightly to accommodate color in the carrier signal[3]. The rest of the world used other systems, the most well-known being Phase Alternating Line (PAL), which remained at 50.00 frames per second[4].

Nowadays, neither analog system remains in use in the developed world. However, the constraints of backwards capability mean that those frame rates remain with us to this day.

---

[3] See https://en.wikipedia.org/wiki/NTSC
[4] See https://en.wikipedia.org/wiki/PAL

1.2.1 Fields vs. Frames

Now, if you've been paying close attention, you will have noticed that in the previous paragraphs, we talked about *frames per second* for cinema, and *fields per second* in the case of television. Are they the same? No, they are not, due to the methods used to present images to the viewer, which are very different between the two technologies.

Traditional film-based cinema double flashes each frame on the screen. Roughly speaking, it presents one frame for 1/48th of a second on the screen, then a rotating disc obscures the image, the image is presented a second time, then the machine pulls on the reel to put the next image to the center of the lens, and the whole cycle begins again. The same principle was used for capture. You can see the disc in the following patent from the Lumiere brothers, marked "j" (fig. 2). This pull-hold-pull mechanism may seem familiar to some. It is based on a sewing machine, which the brothers modified to create their prototype.

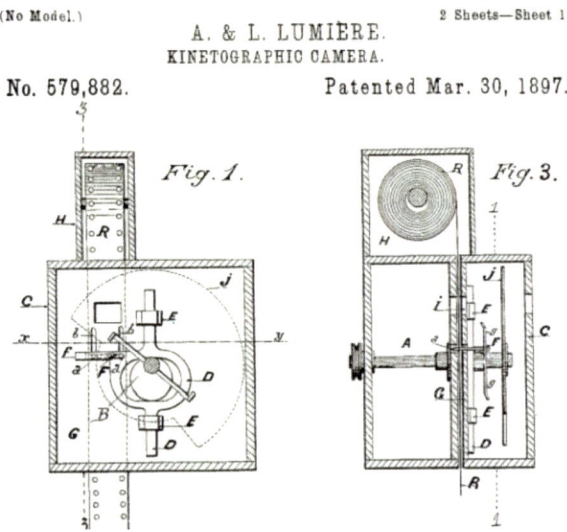

Figure 2 - patent for the Lumière brothers *cinématographe*. Note the semi-circular disc marked "j" which acts as a shutter between the capture of each frame. A similar disc is mounted on the projector.

Television was an analogue, electronic format. Initially, the principle was one-dimensional; a line was drawn, with electrons scanning from left to right, hitting a thin film of *electroluminescent* phosphor deposited on the surface of a vacuum tube. The current intensity dictated how many electrons would hit the screen, hence creating variable *luminance*. Once the electron beam reached the end of the line, it would be shifted vertically for the next line of the image, thus creating a 2D image.

There was not enough bandwidth, originally, to carry the electronic signal through the airwaves at full cycle (60 or 50 Hz depending on the country). Sending 30 or 25 images per second would have solved the issue, but created an uncomfortable flickering effect on the screen, where it would contrast with ambient light (cinema was projected in totally dark rooms and double flashed so the flickering effect was less perceptible).

Engineers found a solution with the concept of *alternating fields*. The first phase of the image scan would cover the odd lines (e.g. lines 1, 3, 5 and so on) at 60 or 50 fields per second, while the second phase of the image would cover the even lines (e.g. lines 2, 4, 6 and so on) 1/60th or 1/50th of a second later. The persistence of luminance on the excited phosphor surface would mean that while one field order was lit, the other one would still be somewhat visible, thus creating the illusion of a full frame image. The first patent for television was filed by Philo T. Farnsworth in 1930 (fig. 3).

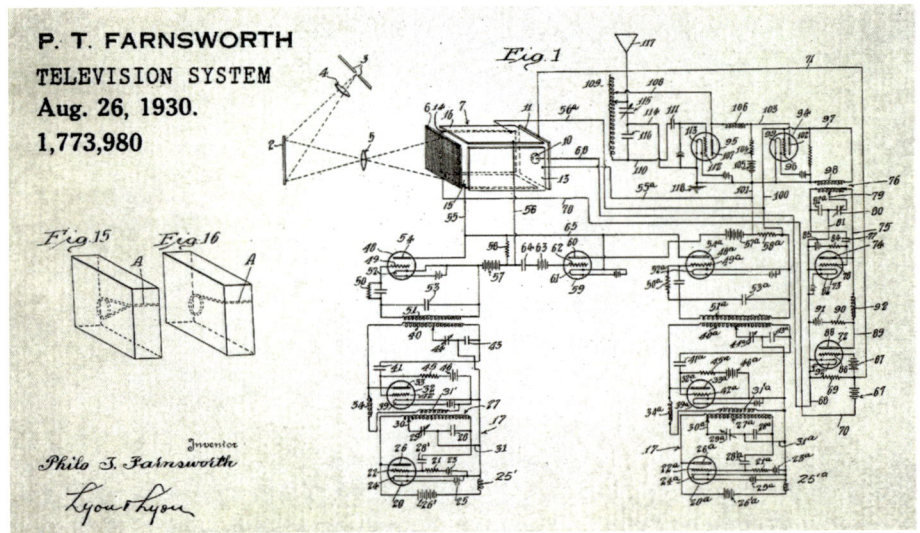

Figure 3 - Television patent by P.T. Farnsworth, 1930.

Today, there is no need for fields as there are no more CRT displays and digital equipment can operate at much higher frame rates. However, images are still broadcast in interlaced format to this day, due once again to backwards compatibility. The last format to support interlaced is High-Definition Television, however; there are no provisions for interlaced in UHD and beyond.

1.2.2 Progressive versus psf

The advent of computers and new imaging technologies in both the motion picture and the television industries allowed for additional frame rates, beyond the original 24 frames and 50/59.94 fields of analog cinema and television. Let's start by discussing the concept of *interlaced* versus *progressive*.

Interlaced used the concept of alternating lines (or fields) in analog television, as we've just covered in the previous paragraphs. Presenting a full frame is called progressive scan, as we are "progressively" building the entire image from top to bottom.

Modern displays like computers, tablets, flat screens, and smartphones all use the progressive format in their image presentation. It is therefore not ideal to present them with interlaced fields. The other progressive format the industry had to deal with was film, and in order to capture progressive film with video systems that were designed for interlaced capture (e.g. magnetic tape recorders), a solution was achieved with the creation of *Progressive, Segmented Frames*, or psf for short. For progressive video, the tape recorder and the medium would keep recording alternating fields, thus not requiring an expensive re-tooling of the production chain, but instead of receiving alternative fields in time, it would receive the odd lines of the first frame, then the even lines of the first frame, and so on. At reconstruction, both fields would be put together to recreate the full frame. It was a bit more complicated for film, which had no multiple of 24 in video equivalent, so a solution using repeating fields was adopted.

1.2.3 3:2 pulldown

The technical challenge with film was to record and present progressive 24fps material in a different time-based interlaced format. The ingenious solution was to alternate two fields of the first frame, three fields of the second frame, two fields of the third frame and three fields of the fourth frame in succession, then repeating the whole cycle for the next four frames. This scheme has been dubbed the 3:2 pulldown (fig. 4) and enabled the capture and playback of 24p in 59.94 fields or 29.97 frames per second.

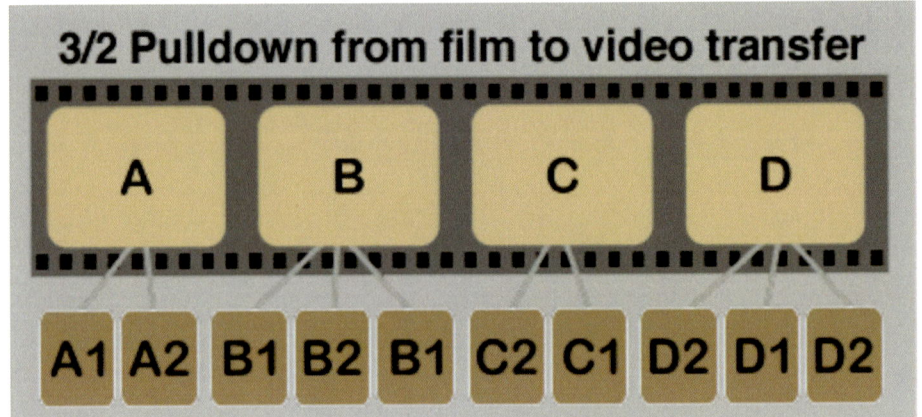

Figure 4 - 3:2 pulldown from 24p to 29.97p or 59.94i
Source: https://mrbetamax.com/3-2Pulldown.htm

As for countries with 50Hz power, they elected to change film speed slightly, adjust sound accordingly and to record the 24 frames in 50 psf, hence lay the frames in a 25fps time base.

1.2.4 High Frame Rate (HFR)

Although not yet deployed, the advent of very powerful processing systems now allows the capture, editing and presentation of content in frame rates higher than ever before. New specifications for UHD TV, for example, will allow for the distribution of 100 and 120fps content, which is considered *High Frame Rate* (HFR) video.

1.2.5 Frame Rate summary

Combining all we learned in this sub-chapter; we can list the following as standardized frame rates used throughout the video and cinema industries:

23.976   Cinema for home (NTSC countries)

24.00   Cinema (Worldwide)

25.00   SD, HD (PAL countries)

29.97   SD, HD (NTSC countries)
50.00   HD and UHD (PAL countries)
59.97   HD and UHD (NTSC countries)
100.0   High Frame Rate (PAL countries)
119.94   HFR (NTSC countries)

1.3 Bit Depth

As the industry transitioned from analog to digital, it was necessary to convert analog formats into bits. Basically, computers today work in ones and zeroes, what we call binary. Analog, on the other side, provides an infinity of values. So how do we fit an infinity of values, say, between completely black and completely white, into a binary system? By grouping ranges of values in discrete "buckets" that are binary, a process that is called *quantizing* (fig. 5).

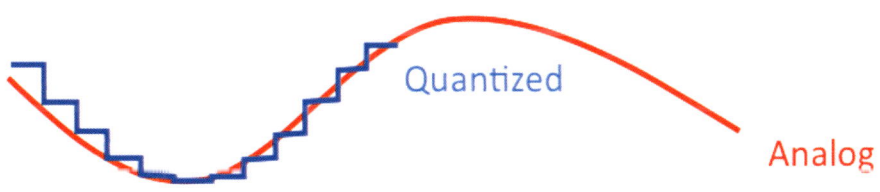

Figure 5 - Quantizing

So, for example, let's say we have a signal that goes between 0 and 100% in analog; we could break down the range of 0 to 100 in increments of 20, which would give us 5 buckets. This is not going to look very representative of the source. If we break it down into increments of 1, this will give us 100 buckets, which is closer to the source. If we break it down into increments of 0.1, we now have 1000 buckets, which is pretty faithful to the original. The number of buckets available is called *bit depth*. Since it's a binary system, the formula is 2 to the power of x as bit depth. For example:

A bit depth of 8 bit = 2 to the power of 8 = 2x2x2x2x2x2x2x2 = 256 "buckets", or levels

10 bits = 2^{10} = 1024 levels
12 bits = 2^{12} = 4096 levels
16 bits = 2^{16} = 65 536 levels

Bit depth is a compromise between faithfulness to the original and file or stream size. Higher bit depths provide better image quality but come at a cost. Cameras that can handle 16-bit per color, for example, require ultra-fast memory cards and fast analog-to-digital converters, adding significantly to the price tag.

The following bit depths are typically used in the video and cinema industry:

 8 bits: Standard Dynamic Range Television
10 bits: High Dynamic Range Television
12 bits: LOG Mastering
16 bits: Linear Mastering

1.3.1 Banding

Let's suppose you are capturing a beautiful sunset. Your eyes see a gradation between the orange-red sun and the blue night sky above. Wonderful, right? For your camera, though, this presents a daunting challenge. There can be hundreds, if not thousands, of shades between the bright orange sun and the dark blue moon. If you do not have enough levels to express those, the frontier between each "bucket" will become apparent on the display. This phenomenon is called *banding* and is typically found in low bitrate images (fig. 6).

Figure 6 - Banding artifacts in low bit depth (top image) versus higher bit depth (bottom)

Remember when we said spatial resolution was not the single factor in assessing image quality? Well, both images in figure 6 have the same spatial resolution. However, as you can see, the lower bit depth of the image on top makes it look much less pleasant than the image below it. It looks downright cheap, as a remnant of past times when computer generated images were produced in ultra-low bit depths.

Now that we understand quantizing, let's look at what exactly is quantized in our digital cameras: the dual properties of light: color and luminance.

1.4 Luminance and Color Resolution

Before we look at how video encodes luminance and color, I believe it is important to understand how our own eyes work.

1.4.1 How our eyes perceive luminance and color

Our eyes do not actually see objects and people. What we see is the reflection of light hitting them, then bouncing back in our eyes. First, light enters the cornea, which is the outer part of the eye (fig. 7). Our pupil contracts or expands to manage different light levels, letting a certain amount of light pass through the crystalline lens, which focuses the light beams on the retina, at the back of our eyes. That phenomenon is what we call accommodation.

On the retina, there is a very small part called the macula (Latin for stain, as it looks like a small spot), where there is a high density of cells that transform colors into electric signals, which are sent by the optic nerve to our visual cortex, the part of the brain that converts this input into images.

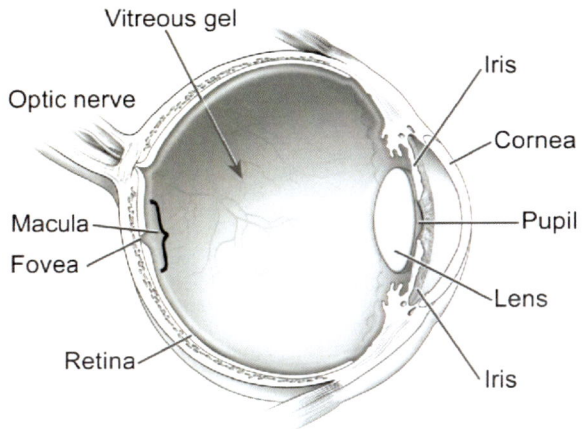

Figure 7 - The Human Eye - by National Eye Institute, National Institutes of Health

The cells that transform light into electrical input are separated in two categories, rods, and cones, due to their peculiar shapes (fig. 8).

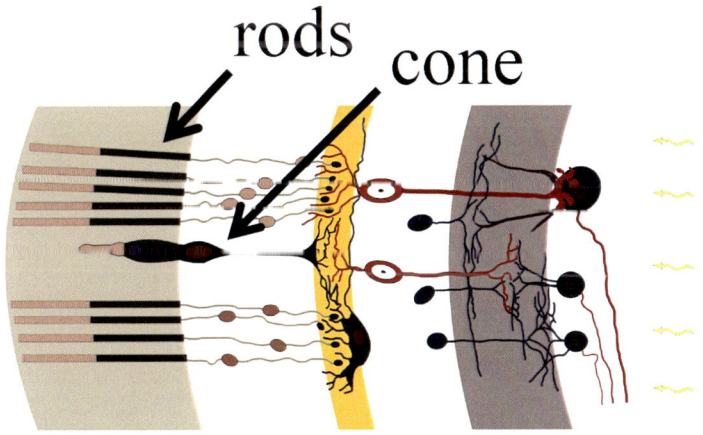

Figure 8 - Section of the retina showing rods and cones - original drawing by Cajal, 1911. Digitized by Chrkl - CC-BY-SA-3.0

Rods are excited by photons from the visible light spectrum, independently of the wavelength - they are therefore more or less color blind. More sensitive to low light than cones, they allow us to see in the dark (which is why everything seems de-saturated at night).

Cones are present in lesser numbers than rods and concentrated mostly in the macula. They require a greater light intensity than rods to function properly. We possess three different types of cones, which react to three ranges of wavelengths - (S)hort, (M)edium and (L)ong, which correspond roughly to the colors blue (at 420 nanometers, or nm), green (at 534 nm), and red (at 564 nm). Our brain uses those three stimuli to interpolate all visible colors. Scientists call this the tri-stimulus model (fig. 9).

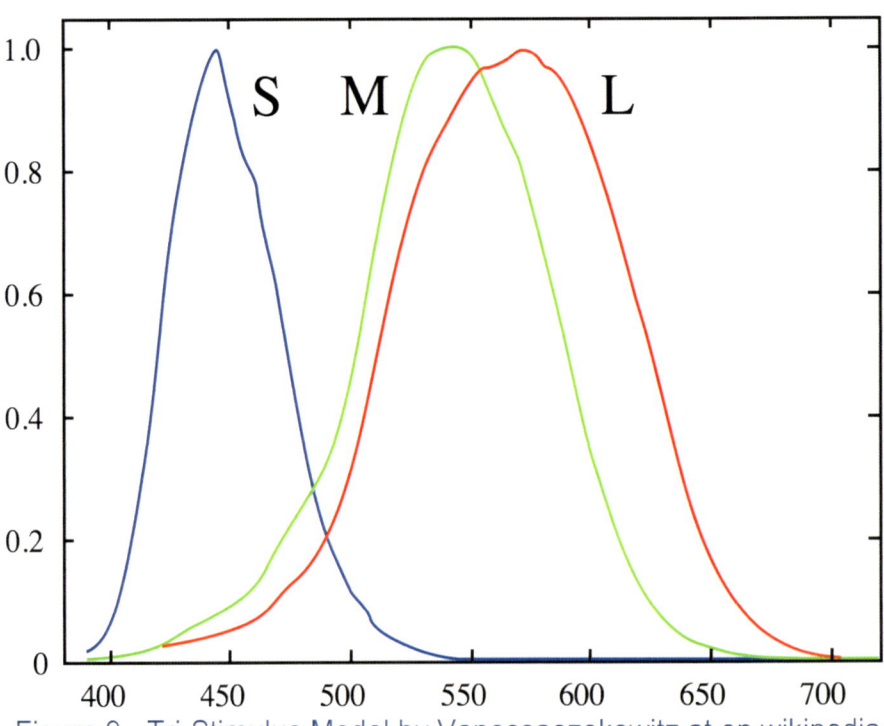

Figure 9 - Tri-Stimulus Model by Vanessaezekowitz at en.wikipedia - CC-BY-SA-3.0

Based on this understanding of how our eyes capture light, scientists built color models and developed technologies to capture and display images based on those three basic colors: (R)ed, G(reen) and B(lue), which correspond to the S, M and L model of the human eye seen above.

The most well-known of those models was created in 1931 by the *Commission Internationale de l'Éclairage* (CIE), or International Lighting Commission, and is based on practical tests. It uses a mathematical model that derives RGB colors (which they call X, Y and Z) in a 2-dimensional figure (x and y axes), which creates the *Color Gamut* of the human eye (fig. 10); in other words, the envelope of colors which human brains can interpolate from the three primary colors perceived by cones (S, M, L). There is a transform that allows us to convert X, Y and Z into S, M and L, but this is for a color science book, a bit out of scope for the current guide.

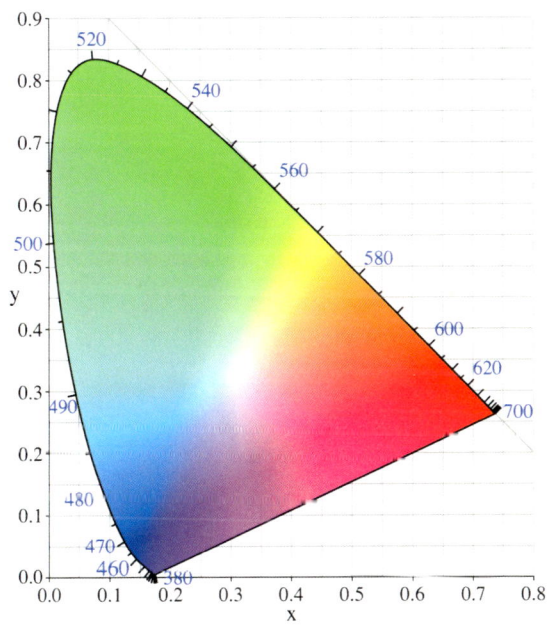

Figure 10 - The CIE 1931 Model (public domain) - wavelength (in nm) in blue

The other axis of the full color model, which is not visible in figure 10, runs perpendicular to the plane of color. It is the luminance of those colors, from lowest to brightest intensity (referred to as the Y axis). So light is represented by a 3-dimensional space (x, y, Y), referred to as the *color volume* (for an example of a color volume, see fig. 11).

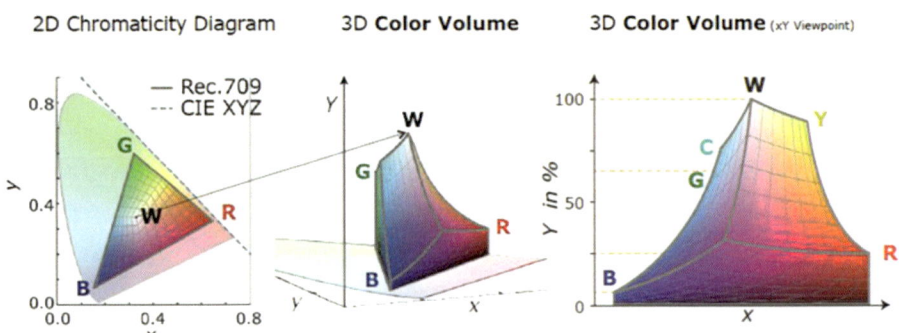

Figure 11 - The REC709 Color Volume - by XBMC Foundation's Kodi media player - www.kodi.tv

1.4.2 How digital cameras perceive light

Like our eyes, modern digital cameras utilize the two main properties of light - waves and particles - to capture images. Consequently, they use two separate types of devices: filters, which separate light waves, giving us color values, and photo-electric cells, transforming photons into electric current, giving us luminance values.

Some digital cameras use prisms to separate incoming light into red, green, and blue, which are then directed to three separate arrays of photoelectric cells. In the older days, those cells were 3-CCD, or Three Charged-Couple Device imagers. Their larger size, more expensive manufacturing, lower readout speed and higher power consumption led to their demise when smaller, faster, and cheaper alternatives were made available, namely CMOS (see next paragraph). 3-CCDs are, nowadays, mostly absent from film and television camera manufacturer lineups.

In 2007, the RED digital cinema company revolutionized the field of digital cinematography by introducing the RED ONE™, a single-chip camera that could capture 4 times the resolution of then state-of-the-art 3-CCD cameras, at a fraction of the cost. At its core, the RED ONE used a single chip, the CMOS (short for Complementary Metal Oxide Semiconductor), with a special array of color filters configured in a Bayer pattern (from the name of its inventor).

Without going deep into the physics of sensors, a CMOS is faster to read out than a CCD, allowing for higher frame rates and larger resolutions; it is less expensive to manufacture, has a smaller footprint and consumes less power, which is why we find the technology in almost every camera, from smartphones to high end cinema.

Figure 12 below illustrates, in a simplified manner, how a CMOS works. Incoming light passes through an infrared (IR) filter, meant to reduce *IR contamination* on the sensor array. This is important as we cannot perceive infrared, but the sensor can, and it would skew color perception if it was not filtered out. Then, light passes through a checkerboard array of color filters arranged in a *Bayer* pattern. It uses a configuration of 2 greens, one blue and one red for each 2x2 pixel block. This does not provide full resolution for the complete image: algorithms are required to interpolate the missing pixels - a process called *Debayering*. So, for a 4K image, we capture approximately 2K of green, 1K of Red and 1K of blue and we let algorithms fill in the blanks to bring back a full 4K of Green, Red and Blue.

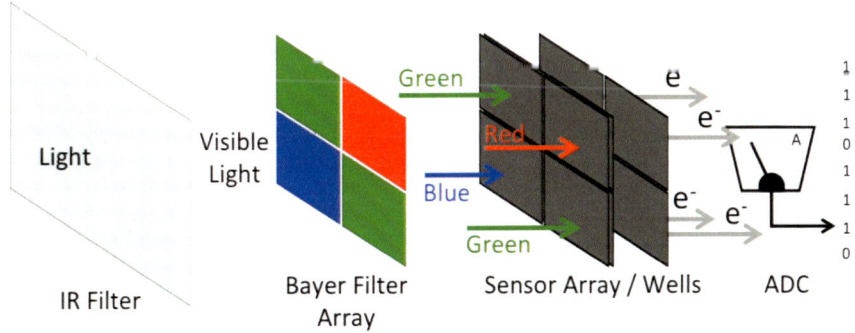

Figure 12 - How a CMOS Sensor Works

Now that the photons are filtered to Red, Green, and Blue wavelengths, they are captured by an array of cells, called photosites. Within those cells, photons hit a silicon layer, displacing electrons, thus creating electrical current. The electrons are accumulated in a "well" during the exposure - called integration time. Then the current is measured, and the process begins again for the next frame.

So far, what I have described is an analog process. The digital part happens when we take the current measurements and convert them, through an ADC, or *Analog to Digital Converter*, into a limited set of digital values, which will be interpreted as luminance for the three primary colors.

To summarize, digital sensors filter light waves to capture the three primary colors, and then convert photons into electrons, which are digitized to provide light intensity.

1.4.3 Color representation in Video production

What we have seen so far are the SML (human vision) and RGB (cameras, displays) models of color representation. There are, however, many other ways to represent color. A good primer on color science[5] will explain those in detail to readers interested in the mathematics behind; however, as this is a fundamentals overview, we will just list some of the most used models and their application in the TV and cinema industry:

RGB: Red, Green, Blue   Camera capture
YUV: Luma(Y) Blue (U) Red (V)   Uncompressed Video
YCbCr: Luma (Y) Blue minus luma (Cb) Red minus luma (Cr)
                                                                         Digital Video
ICtCp: Luma (I) Blue-Yellow (Ct) Red-Green (Cb)   HDR

---

[5] You could start here: https://en.wikipedia.org/wiki/Color_space

1.4.4 Color Spaces in Video for Television and Cinema

As of this publication, there is not a single display technology that allows the reproduction of the entire CIE 1931 model. Therefore, what we are working with are color spaces that are subsets of the full color spectrum that humans can see. A color space is typically defined by its Red, Green, and Blue boundaries of representation. The combination of all possible R, G and B values provide the full spectrum of color representation within this color space, something called *Color Gamut*.

In traditional color television, the color space (standardized as *International Telecommunications Union, Radiocommunication Sector, Broadcasting service, Television, standard number 709*, or ITU-R BT.709 for short[6]) boundaries were created with the maximum color reproducible with red, green, and blue phosphors back in the day of *CRT* television. Although those are no longer manufactured nor present in the modern display ecosystem, we still live with those restrictive boundaries in Standard Dynamic Range, High-Definition Television to this day.

For cinema, the *Digital Cinema Initiatives* consortium elected to emulate the color space of film print, as far as could be achieved with the digital technology of the early 2000, that is, Texas Instruments' *Digital Micromirror Device* (DMD for short), with a Xenon lamp as an illuminant. This was standardized as the DCI P3 color space[7].

With the advent of Ultra-High Definition, the Consumer Electronics industry wanted to adopt a wider color space, more in line with the capabilities of the best modern display devices of the day. After much deliberation, they decided to use RGB laser projection primaries as the boundaries of their color space, which was standardized as BT.2020[8] (fig. 13).

---

[6] See https://en.wikipedia.org/wiki/Rec._709
[7] See https://en.wikipedia.org/wiki/DCI-P3
[8] See https://en.wikipedia.org/wiki/Rec._2020

BT.709

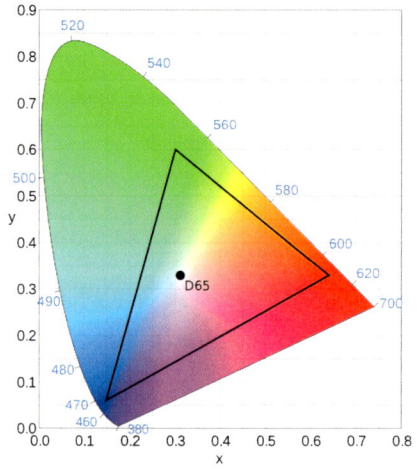

DCI P3

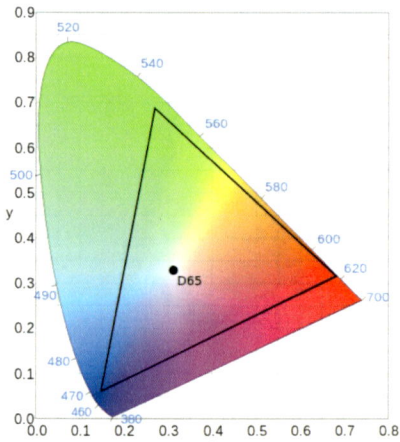

BT.2020

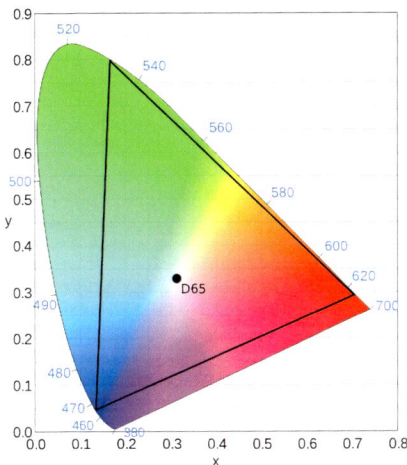

Figure 13 - BT.709, DCI P3 and BT.2020 Color spaces. Note the limited area covered by BT.709 versus BT.2020

1.4.5 Chroma sub-sampling

To save bandwidth, some color representations will remove part of the color information. Color sub-sampling is more prevalent in broadcast (where physical transmission is always a compromise due to the limited electromagnetic spectrum allocation to broadcast waves) than cinema (where image integrity is valued at a premium and there are no broadcasting requirements).

As our eyes are significantly more sensitive to changes in luminance than changes in color, it is possible to use sub-sampling to reduce the overall size of an image without affecting quality significantly[9]. The most well-known color sub-sampling scheme is the 4:X:X, where the first digit corresponds to sample size (block of 4 pixels), the second and third one corresponding to the first and second row of the blocks of pixels, as described below (fig. 14):

---

[9] See https://en.wikipedia.org/wiki/Chroma_subsampling

Figure 14 - Chroma sub-sampling in Broadcast Video

4:4:4 means that for a 4-pixel block, we are using all color information from the first row (4) and the second row (4) of pixels.

4:2:2 means that out of the 4-pixel block, only two pixels of color are preserved; the first and third pixels of the first (2) and second row (2).

4:2:0 means that out of the 4-pixel block, only two pixels of color are kept; for example, the first and third pixels of the first row and none of the pixels of the second row.

This may seem radical, but in a well-balanced image, it is hard for the viewer to perceive color sub-sampling, as the eye is more sensitive to shifts in luminance than color and colors typically don't change drastically between adjacent pixels.

1.4.6 Transfer Functions: EOTF, OETF, OOTF

Now that we've covered color, let's have a look at the other dimension of light, which is intensity, or luminance. As we have covered before, luminance is perceived when photons excite light receptors in our eyes.

Cameras capture luminance by measuring the current generated by electrons displaced by photons during integration (see section 1.4.2).

As light is captured at the source, it is digitized and given code values according to the camera's bit depth, as well as a certain *transfer function*, which determines how code values are allocated. This is called an *Opto-Electric (or electronic) Transfer Function*, or OETF for short.

When we want to see the light intensity, another transfer function, the *Electro-Optical Transfer Function*, or EOTF, is applied. It converts code values into luminance for the display.

The entire process is the summation of OETF and EOTF, what is called the *Opto-Optical Transfer Function*, or OOTF for short. The process (what is often called "glass to glass" in the industry) is not 100% faithful. No display device to this day can cover the intensity range we may encounter in nature.

Figure 15 below illustrates the OOTF of traditional television. Readers who wish to further their understanding of transfer functions are invited to read our other Digital Troublemaker Guide, *HDR for Motion Pictures and Television*.

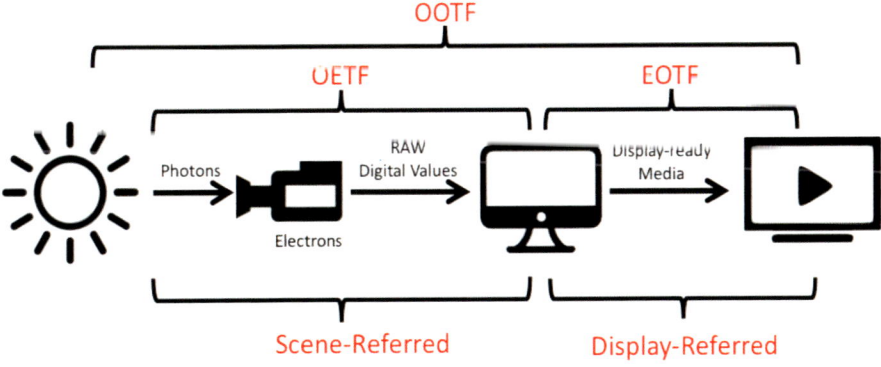

Figure 15 - Relationship between OETF, EOTF and OOTF

The transfer function for High-Definition Television is, once again, a legacy from the days of CRT television. It takes the form of a power function, called Gamma[10]. This is covered in the BT.709 standard, and the EOTF applies a gamma correction of 2.4 to bring luminance back to what a display can accept (fig. 16). The overall OOTF in HDTV is relative to the peak brightness of the display. In traditional CRT, it was covering only from 0 to 100 cd/m^2, or candela per meter squared, the metric unit of illuminance for a display.

Current Standard Dynamic Range displays typically go up to 250-300 cd/m^2 or even higher. To give you an idea of scale, the light intensity outside on a sunny day can exceed 30 000 cd/m^2.

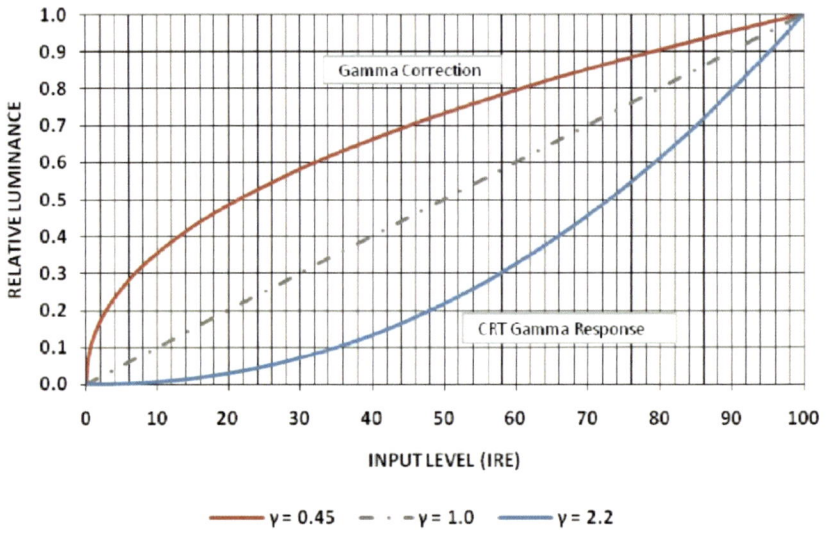

Figure 16 - Gamma response in traditional CRT versus Gamma correction - still used to this day in digital displays

As the industry moves towards High Dynamic Range (or HDR for short), the OOTFs are becoming much larger, typically covering up to 10 000 cd/m^2 for PQ, which prescribes a pre-determined transfer function (see

---

[10] See https://en.wikipedia.org/wiki/Rec._709

below); for HLG, which is a relative transfer function like Gamma was, it goes up to screen max luminance (which is around 1000 cd/m² in current generation displays).

1.4.6.1 Hybrid Log-Gamma (HLG) Transfer Function

HLG[11] is a standard OETF suggested by the public broadcasters BBC and NHK. It is a relative transfer function, which means that the EOTF will map code values generated in the OETF to a certain percentage of the display's peak luminance. Therefore, if a display can generate up to 1000 cd/m² of intensity, a 100% signal will generate that value on the screen. If the display can only display up to 600 cd/m², that is the value it will provide at 100% signal intensity.

1.4.6.2 Perceptual Quantizer (PQ) Transfer Function

PQ[12], which was later standardized as *ST.2084*, was developed by Dolby Laboratories with the intent to provide an absolute OOTF that closely matches human perception of shifts in luminance. Its EOTF is fixed, which means that CVs are not displayed relatively to the screen's peak luminance. Its CVs cover all luminance values up to 10 000 cd/m², which corresponds to 100% signal.

If a pixel's code value exceeds a display's maximum peak luminance, the displayed luminance will *clip*, meaning it will be displayed at maximum intensity and show no detail.

---

[11] See https://en.wikipedia.org/wiki/Hybrid_log%E2%80%93gamma
[12] See https://en.wikipedia.org/wiki/Perceptual_quantizer

1.4.6.3 Vendor-Specific Transfer Functions (VLog, SLog, LogC, CLog, etc.)

There is a plethora of OETFs that were developed by camera manufacturers with the intent of capturing as much dynamic range as the cameras allow while using as little bit depth as possible. Those include Panasonic VLog, Sony's SLog (fig. 17), Arri's LogC and Canon CLog. As each of those TFs has different exposure specifications, it is imperative that the user understands and respects exposure levels when using them, to produce the best possible images.

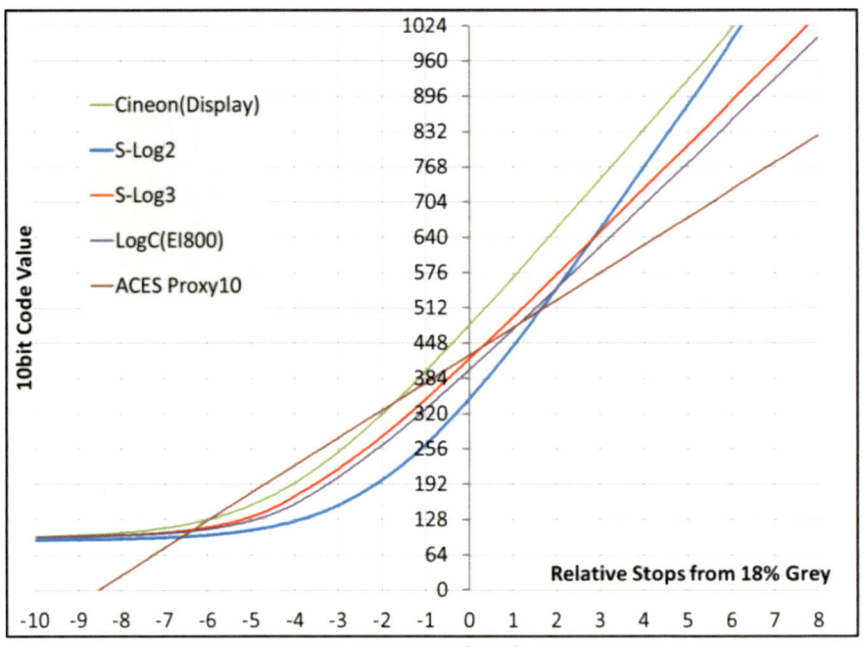

Figure 17 - Sony S-Log 2, 3, Cineon, Arri LogC and ACES Transfer Functions

In general, those are meant to be converted to multiple EOTFs at the time of color grading and not to be seen "as is" during the post-production process. They are scene-referred, not display-referred.

1.4.6.4 Scene linear, scene-referred, and display-referred

At capture, an OETF can take one of three forms: Scene linear, scene referred, or display referred.

Scene linear means that the OETF is providing equal range to each code value in its transfer function. Therefore, 50% of signal equals to 50% of code value. 20% of signal equals to 20% of code value, etc.

To prevent banding artifacts, a scene linear encoding requires a lot of code values. In cinema, the preferred bit depth for scene-linear is 16-bit, or 65 536 CVs per color to cover the range. Multiply it three times to cover all luminance values for Red, Green, and Blue and you will get trillions of possible combinations, avoiding banding in any condition.

Scene Referred means that the OETF is in direct relationship to capture, but each code value does not hold an equal part of the overall dynamic range. As our eyes are more sensitive to changes in luminance in the lower part of the range, CVs cover less range there than in highlights. This allows vendors to lower the bit rate while preventing visible banding artifacts. Typically, scene-referred formats use 12 bits, or 4096 code values per color to cover the range.

Display Referred means that the code values were designed with the intended display format in mind. This is a destructive operation, as it means an inverse cannot be applied to return to the scene values. In television, display-referred formats typically use either 8 bits (256 levels per color) in BT.709 or 10 bits (1024 levels per color) in BT.2020.

Some software does not indicate bit depth, but instead uses the monikers *millions, billions, and trillions of colors*. This is very approximate, and bit depth should be used instead, whenever possible, to get the true numbers.

1.5 Putting it all together

We now have a complete understanding of what constitutes a fully uncompressed image (fig. 18), that is, the combination of:

- Spatial resolution, in pixels
- Temporal resolution, in frames per second
- Color Space, in one of the models we've covered
- Transfer Function, in one of the functions we've covered
- Color representation
- Bit Depth

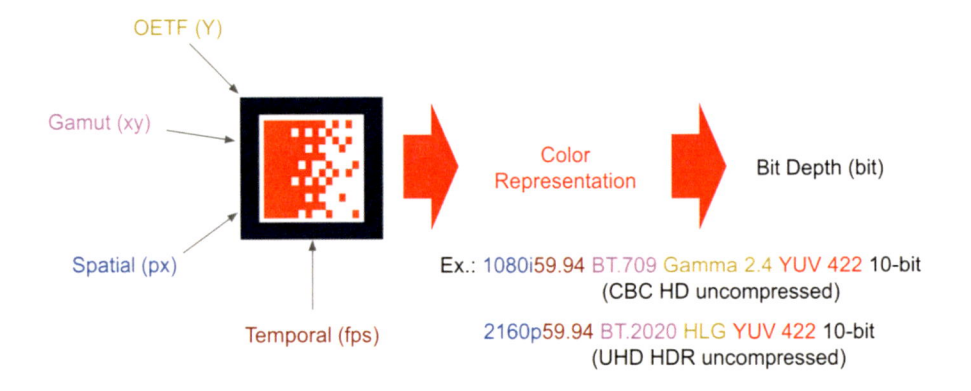

Figure 18 - What constitutes a full, uncompressed image

In the example above, we can decipher the long description as follows:

2160p	UHD resolution at 3840 x 2160, progressive frames
59.94	NTSC-based frame rate of 59.94 frames per second
BT.2020	Color space for Wide Color Gamut (WCG)
HLG	Hybrid Log-Gamma Transfer Function
YUV	Video color representation
422	Color sub-sampling
10-bit	Bit Depth

This example happens to be describing uncompressed Broadcast Ultra-High Definition with High Dynamic Range. For High-Definition Broadcast, it would be:

1080i59.94 BT.709 Gamma 2.4 YUV 422 8-bit

1080i	Interlaced HD resolution at 1920 x 1080
59.94	59.94 *fields* per second
BT.709	HD color space
Gamma 2.4	HD transfer function
YUV	Video color representation
422	Color sub-sampling
8-bit	Bit Depth

2. Video Compression and Decompression

So far, we have looked at everything that comprises video resolution. If we stopped there, we could not have developed the industry the way it has evolved, as computing and storage requirements would be economically and, often, technologically impossible to meet.

Enter the world of *codecs*, which make the magic possible. The word codec is a contraction of the words COmpression and DECoding. It is how we can shrink file and stream sizes by several orders of magnitude, making it possible to do so many of the things we take for granted today, like streaming video on a laptop, capturing clips on a smartphone, broadcasting hundreds of channels on the air, etc.

Codecs are used for a variety of purposes. Some are more specialized in capture, some are suited to post-production work (tasks like editing, visual effects, etc.) while others are tailored to meet the demand of millions of streaming users.

Each codec is built on a series of compromises, trying to get the maximum out of the following requirements:

- Image quality
- Image size
- Computing speed and power

Codecs designed for mass streaming of few assets, for example, will be more tolerant of heavy computing if it means that the file will be smaller, and thus save a maximum of bandwidth. Codecs such as AV1, which we will discuss later, belong to this category. On the opposite side, live capture codecs for production are typically designed to require less complex computing, to allow processing in real time. This is the case, for example, for video over IP in the ST.2110 standard[13].

There are several families of codecs; they are based on their technical principles. In order to discuss codecs in depth, we would require an entire book; as this is a fundamentals manual, we will simplify and focus on major characteristics of the most popular families of codecs so the reader can understand general principles, not the intricate details.

2.1 Lossless codecs

The first category of codecs, lossless, maintain complete data integrity. The way they reduce size is by reducing the storage of redundant information. While this is ideal from an image quality standpoint, these codecs are only marginally effective in reducing file size, as modern images contain very little redundancy. My colleague Frans De jong from the European Broadcast Union compares this to a sponge. You can squeeze it to reduce its size but release it and it gets back to its full shape with no loss.

In this family of codecs, we find the familiar ZIP format as well as the PIZ format, used for OpenEXR image sequences (see the Digital Troublemaker Guide *HDR for Motion Pictures and Television* for more information)

2.2 Lossy codecs

This category encompasses all the codecs that destroy, at least partially, the source information. In other words, you cannot reverse the process and reconstruct the source file without losing some data. Depending on the need, some of those codecs can be visually lossless

---

[13] ST.2110 standardizes high quality audiovisual production infrastructures based on the widely used IP network technology, instead of specialized video infrastructures.

to the untrained eye, all the way to low bandwidth robust codecs that are always transmitting an image although that image clearly looks degraded. This is the type of aggressive codecs used, for example, in videoconferencing applications, where the need to keep the connection is greater than the subjective evaluation of image quality.

Following the sponge analogy, it is like if we hollowed the inside of the sponge. It superficially looks the same but is significantly reduced in mass. If you push the thinning too far, the walls of the sponge would collapse, just like aggressive compression can destroy image quality.

Within the greater family of lossy codecs, two types emerge: *Intra-frame*, and *Inter-frame* codecs. Intra-frame codecs will try to compress the video in an image-by-image fashion; basically, they treat each frame as an independent image and base their computations on the content of each frame. So, in essence, inter-frame codecs are strictly using spatial resolution to compress.

Inter-frame codecs are more complex and combine an analysis of spatial and temporal resolution to perform compression. In other words, they will identify similarities in consecutive frames in time and eliminate those similarities, focusing on the difference from frame to frame. This yields much smaller files than intra-frame codecs, albeit at the cost of having to analyze several frames in a sequence to compute encoding decisions.

Figure 19 below illustrates, in a simplified manner, the difference between intra-frame and inter-frame compression:

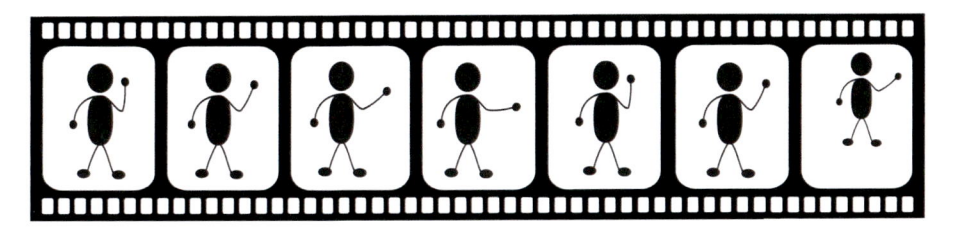

Intraframe Compression
Every frame is encoded Individually

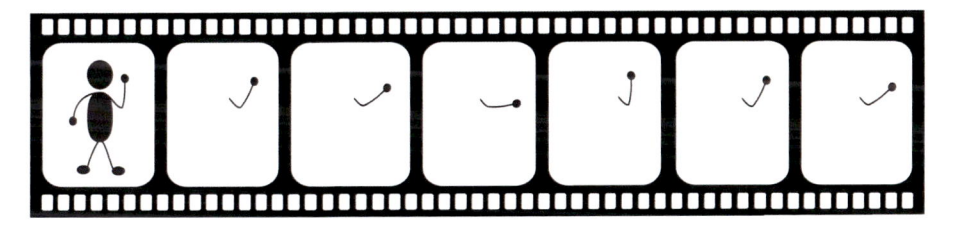

Interframe Compression
Only the differences between frames are encoded for each group of frames

Figure 19 - Intra versus Inter frame compression
https://www.bhphotovideo.com/explora/video/tips-andsolutions/things-you-wanted-to-know-about-compression-butwere-afraid-to-ask

2.2.1 I, P and B frames

Within interframe compression, there are three major types of frames: I, P and B[14]. I stands for Intra-frame, a frame that does not need any other frames to be decoded. While this is the case for every frame in Intra-frame compression, it is just encompassing the first and last frame of a Group Of Pictures, or GOP, in Inter-frame compression.

The second type of frame, in inter-frame compression, is the P frame, where P stands for Predictive. This type of frame uses information from the previous frame(s) to predict motion in the current frame. This reduces file size as what is estimated to be redundant information gets discarded. To decode a P frame, the previous frame(s) need to have been previously decoded, naturally.

---

[14] See https://en.wikipedia.org/wiki/Video_compression_picture_types

Finally, the last main type of frame in inter-frame compression is the B frame, where B stands for Bi-directional. This type of frame uses information from previous AND following frame(s) to achieve even further reduction in size (fig. 20).

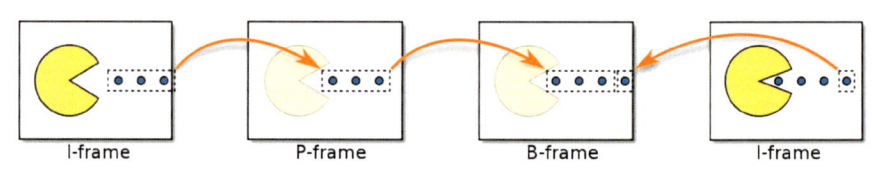

Figure 20 - I, P and B frames
https://en.m.wikipedia.org/wiki/File:I_P_and_B_frames.svg

Looking at figure 20, we can see that the first and last frame are complete (intra-frame compression) and can be decoded without any context. The second picture from the left is a prediction based on the first picture. Since the character is not estimated to be in motion, it does not need to be encoded; the codec will only encode the moving dots. The third picture in the sequence is a bi-directional frame. It looks at previous as well as following frames (in this case a full intra-frame) and determines that it needs to encode the difference between the two, which is even smaller in size. Thus, a combination of I, P and B frames allow for a significant reduction in file size.

The downside of inter-frame compression is that it requires more memory and processing. The information about previous and following frames needs to be stored in memory to make the calculations during compression. Similarly, a buffer is required at decompression to rebuild a full image from the P and B frames.

If, during transmission, one of the I frames is corrupted and cannot be read, the whole GOP will be affected and significant portions of the image will be missing and/or wrong, until the next I frame appears and the full image is reconstructed (fig. 21).

Figure 21 - Correct intra frame (left) versus corrupted frame in a GOP (right)

Together, a combination of I, P and B frames create a cyclic group of pictures. This is the basis behind several modern codecs like H.264, that use what we call Long-GOP, or *Long Group-Of-Pictures* (fig. 22).

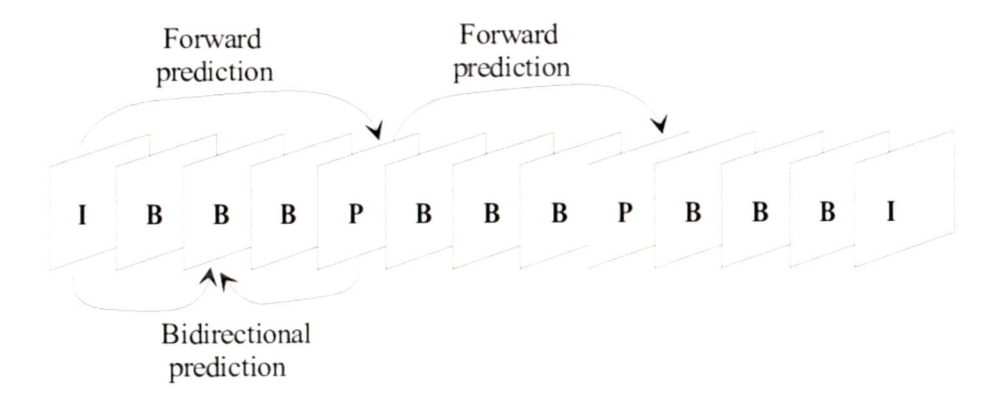

Figure 22 - Long GOP with I, P and B frames

2.2.2 Codec trade-offs

As stated at the beginning of this chapter, each codec is a compromise between image quality, file size and computing requirements. It is therefore not an accident that we have a plethora of codecs in use -

each of them has a particular niche application, or market, demanding either smaller size or faster processing.[15]

Figure 23 illustrates where some of the most popular current codecs are situated on the complexity to file size scale. On the left of the scale, we find intra-frame, low complexity codecs like Jpeg XS. While they generate significantly larger file sizes, their low complexity allows for live capture, transport, and display of images without introducing significant latency. This is one of the main reasons why those codecs are used in live transport protocols like ST.2110 (see chapter 3.2.1.1).

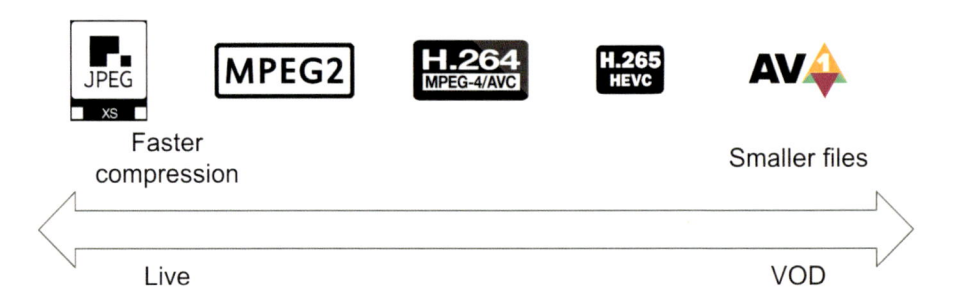

Figure 23 - Codec complexity Vs. File size

At the opposite end of the scale, we find inter-frame, high complexity codecs like AV1. While they require significant processing power for compression, the payback is a much smaller file size, making them ideal for *Over-The-Top* (OTT) streaming services, who may distribute the same file millions of times during its life cycle.

In between those two extremes, we find more "balanced" codecs, offering reasonable complexity and file size, like H.264. Those "Swiss army knife" codecs are generally used for the production and post-production of broadcast assets, making them well suited for digital cameras, editorial software, and playout devices.

---

[15] There are also legal and financial implications in codec selection due to licensing schemes which vary greatly.

In general, the following are the codecs you might encounter more frequently in the industry as of the publication of this guide:

MPEG2 (XDCam)   Broadcast, cable, satellite, DVD
H.264 (AVC, XAVC) Camera capture, post-production
H.265 (HEVC)   Consumer and prosumer capture
JPEG 2000/XS   Ultra low latency IP live video
AV1   On-demand streaming

2.3 Packaging - Video Containers

At this point, we now have our (more or less) compressed video. This is not enough, however, to distribute content to viewers. We are missing the audio component, as well as additional data like time of capture, sub-titles, file name, etc. All this information is aggregated in what we call a "container". The package contains:

- Source Video and Audio (called *essences*)
- Additional data (called *metadata*)

The most common containers you will encounter in video are:

MPEG TS   Stands for *Motion Picture Expert Group - Transport Stream*. The format currently used in receivers (or set-top-box) at home and transported via cable, satellite, and digital terrestrial broadcast.

MXF   Stands for M*edia eXchange Format*.   Typically found in broadcast post-production workflows

MOV   Apple Quicktime container.   Typically found in episodic and indie film post-production workflows

MP4   Stands for MPEG-4. Typically found in consumer cameras, as well as social media assets

DCP   Stands for *Digital Cinema Package*. The container for theatrical assets like motion pictures.

2.4 Putting it all together

2.4.1 Encoding and packaging with Adobe Media Encoder™

Adobe Media Encoder (AME) simplifies the compression and packaging processes by allowing the user to select from a drop-down menu containing the most popular presets in the industry. The main interface of AME (fig. 24) consists of three main windows: A media selector window (top left), a preset window (bottom left) and a rendering queue (right).

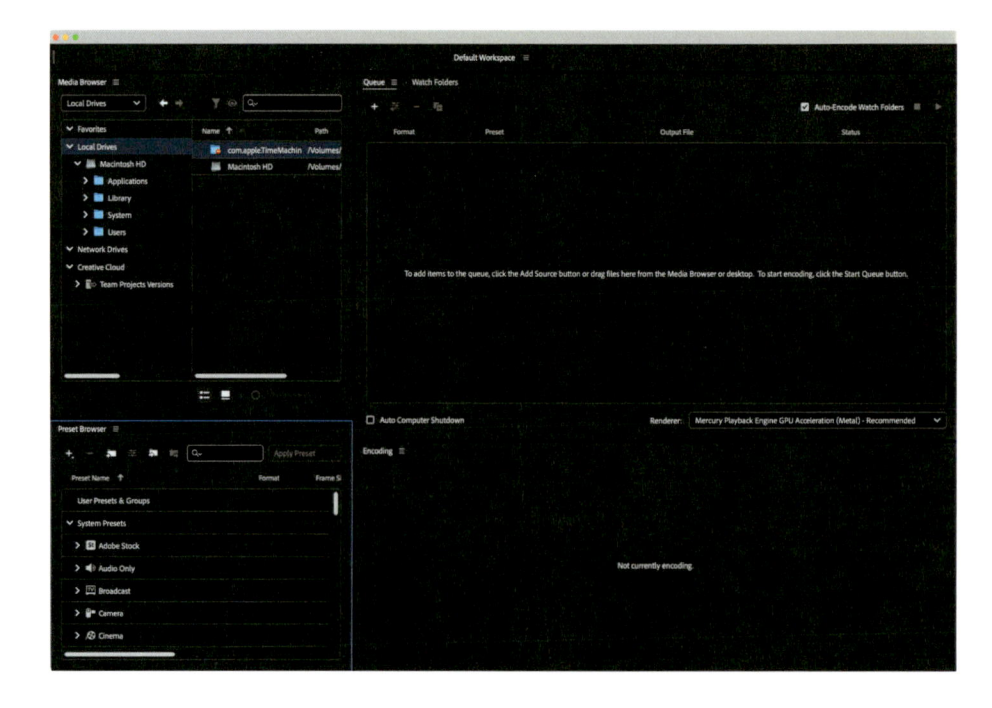

Figure 24 - AME Graphic User Interface (GUI)

After selecting a media in the browser window, or simply drag and dropping it in the render window, the user selects a package in the preset window and drops it on the media in the render queue, then presses the play button (top right corner), and voilà! A conform package is created from the source assets.

Media Encoder can also be set to automatically create packages from a system folder, what is referred to in the industry as a *drop folder* (i.e. you drop your files in the folder and the system automatically processes them).

There are many pros to using AME as an encoder and a packager, but the monthly subscription model may not be suitable for all budgets and those who have intermittent needs. We will therefore look at alternatives that allow you to start practicing without having to spend any money.

2.4.2 Encoding and packaging with HandBrake

Handbrake is one of the most popular prosumer solutions on the market, for good reason. Outside of its unbeatable price (provided free of charge under a General Public License Agreement), it has a decent GUI (fig. 25) and encodes most of the popular production - and independent - formats. Several professionals in the industry will use it to transcode exotic or broken consumer-originated files into broadcast ready assets, as it excels at pushing encode through even in the case where headers are defective, or several packets are missing.

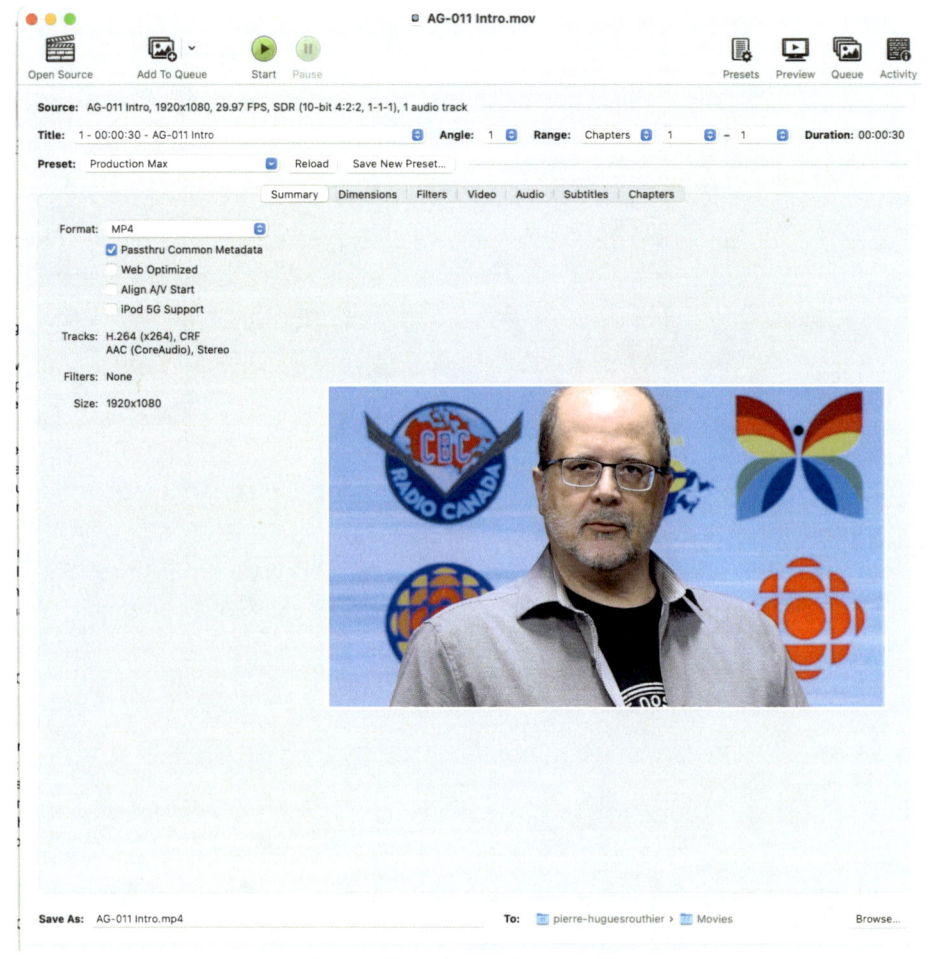

Figure 25 - Handbrake GUI

As with AME, HandBrake offers a menu of presets. Although this one is more geared towards the amateur and prosumer, presets can be fine-tuned by the professional with the use of tabs, allowing the customization of codec, resizing, special filters (e.g. de-interlacing), video and audio formats, subtitles and… chapters, a legacy of its DVD-era code.

Detailed instructions and the GUI itself can be downloaded from the site https://handbrake.fr/ free of charge. There is also an extensive community that is accessible as well as a GitHub repository on the same site.

2.4.3 Encoding and packaging with DaVinci Resolve™

Professional users working in the film and high-end episodic industry will often rely on Blackmagic's DaVinci Resolve to encode their packages, which are geared towards a different market, with DCP and DolbyVision features aimed at the Netflixes and film studios of this world.

For those that want to take a look, a free version of Resolve that can be downloaded here:
https://www.blackmagicdesign.com/products/davinciresolve

As the software is quite complex and aimed at professional colorists, it is strongly recommended to get formal training if you are interested in Resolve.

2.4.4 Validating the package

Now that we have compressed our file with video and audio essences, plus added metadata, and put all of this in a package, we can use a visualization tool to ensure all the information is accurate. One of several tools available to accomplish this task is *MediaInfo*[16], an open-source piece of software designed specifically for that. Here is what the interface looks like (fig. 24).

---

[16] MediaInfo web site: https://mediaarea.net/en/MediaInfo

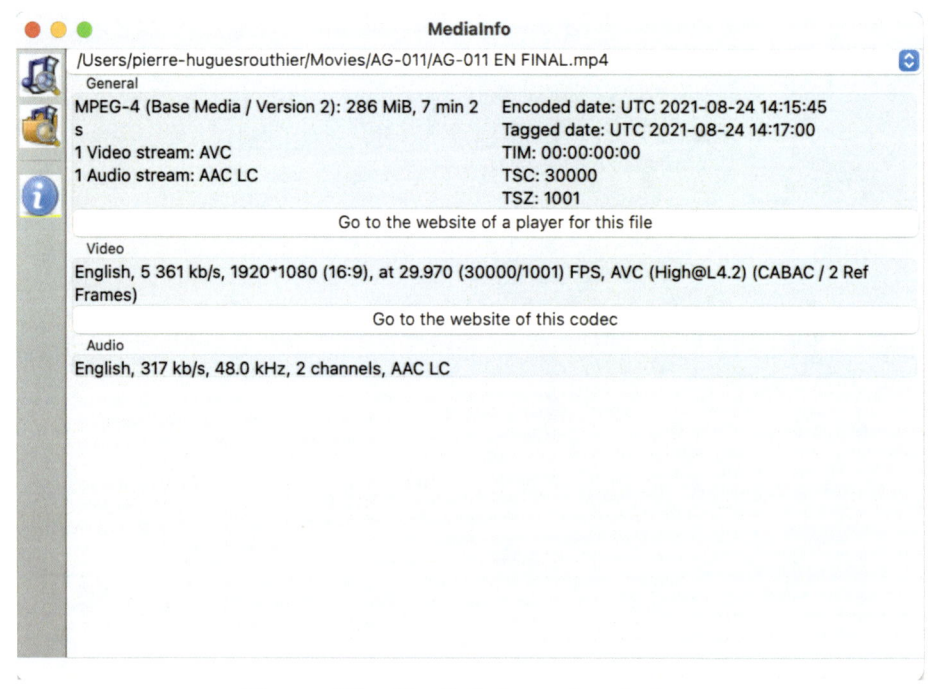

Figure 24 - MediaInfo main window

On the left-hand side, by clicking on one of the first two icons, the user can select a file or a folder for analysis. In figure 24, we see the result of selecting a file, in minimal view. For a more complete view, I recommend using the setting *HTML* in the *View* top menu. It will format all information about the file in an easier to read fashion (fig. 25).

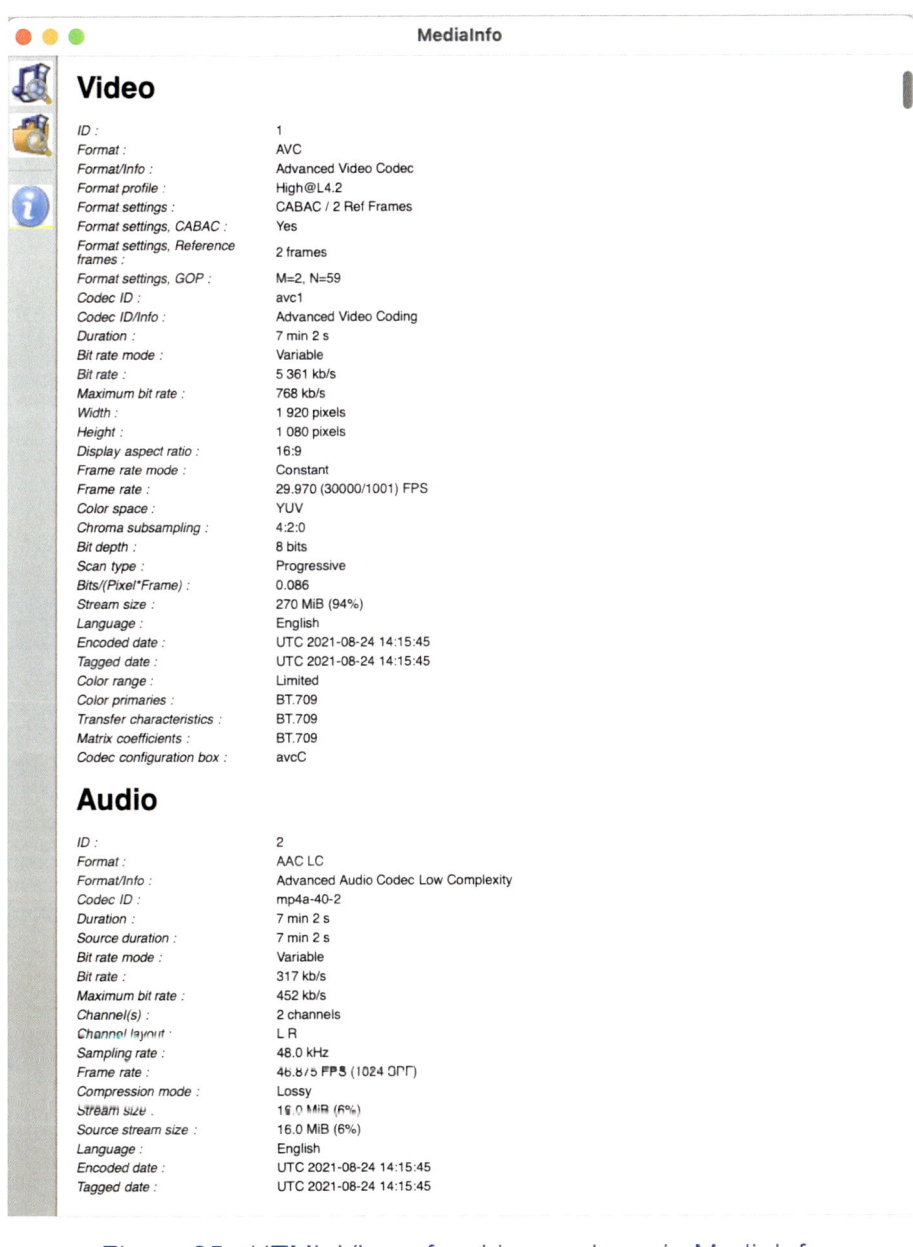

Figure 25 - HTML View of a video package in MediaInfo

There is a ton of information in this view about the file we're looking at. For example, we see that we have a GOP structure, with the distance between two intraframes (GOP "N" value) of 59 frames.

As the frame rate for this file is 29.97 fps, this means that the length of each GOP is approximately 2 seconds.

Most of the information in this view refers to sections we've covered in this guide, like spatial, temporal, color space, transfer function, sub-sampling, bit depth, etc.

The window also informs us about the format and compression of the audio essence, which is sync with the video track, as well as additional metadata (fig. 26).

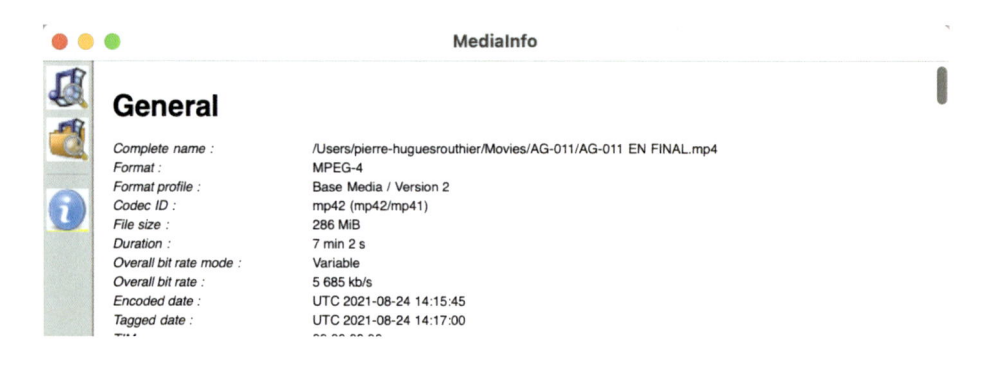

```
                            MediaInfo

General
Complete name :         /Users/pierre-huguesrouthier/Movies/AG-011/AG-011 EN FINAL.mp4
Format :                MPEG-4
Format profile :        Base Media / Version 2
Codec ID :              mp42 (mp42/mp41)
File size :             286 MiB
Duration :              7 min 2 s
Overall bit rate mode : Variable
Overall bit rate :      5 685 kb/s
Encoded date :          UTC 2021-08-24 14:15:45
Tagged date :           UTC 2021-08-24 14:17:00
```

Figure 26 - General File information metadata in MediaInfo

2.5 Source, Mezzanine and Distribution formats

In general, assets will go through three generations, if you want, of formats: Source, Mezzanine and Distribution.

2.5.1 Source Assets

These are assets that are in the native capture device format. Depending on the type of production and post-production lead-times and budgets, source assets can vary from RAW all the way to highly compressed, display-referred formats.

2.5.2 Mezzanine

Once post-production (editorial, color, etc.) is completed, assets are rendered in a new file, typically in a higher bitrate than what will be distributed: the *Mezzanine* format.

The rationale behind the mezzanine format is to have an asset with sufficient resolution and bit depth to serve all distribution needs. For example, it would be very time consuming to re-render from source assets a high bitrate version for television, a medium bitrate version for the web and a low bitrate version in several different resolutions for social media. Instead, the edit will be rendered once from the source assets in the mezzanine format, then multiple down-scale and transcodes can be performed from that rendered mezzanine, which is much more efficient and frees post-production resources to work on other content instead of transcoding.

2.5.3 Distribution

Distribution files are typically compressed and tailored to a specific outlet (e.g. HD television, social media, proprietary Web service, smartphone app, etc.). As stated before, it is a smart strategy to start from a mezzanine format to generate all those versions to free post resources. Another way to increase efficiency is to use automation solutions which use presets and batch processing to convert mezzanine files in several distribution formats automatically.

Distribution assets are typically meant to be viewed "as is". Their heavy compression means that using them for archival and future post-production is not recommended.

2.6 Common Industry Bitrates and Formats

The sections below briefly describe some of the common distribution formats that can be found in the industry. This list is intended to give an idea of the process but is far from exhaustive.

2.6.1 Mpeg-2

This is the historical format for broadcast in digital High-Definition Television (HDTV) for several broadcasters. Its mezzanine is comprised of an mpeg-2 package in MXF format at 50Mbps in 8-bit, a format branded by Sony as XDCamHD. For contrast, distribution in mpeg-2 for this mezzanine will typically be between 4 and 10 Mbps.

2.6.2 H.264

This is a format that is frequently used for 1080p, web and on-demand distribution. Its mezzanine is comprised of an H.264 package in MXF or MP4 format at 100Mbps in 10-bit, a format branded by Sony as XAVC I100. For contrast, distribution in H.264 for this mezzanine will typically be between 2.5 and 10 Mbps.

2.6.3 Social Media

Different Social Media platforms use different bitrates and allow the import of several packages and codecs. Typically, here are some of the formats that will be encountered for distribution:

- Youtube: 1080p or 720p, H.264, MP4, 16Mbps, 8-bit
- Facebook: 1080p or 720p, H.264, MP4, 12Mbps, 8-bit
- X (Twitter): 1080p, H.264, MP4, 6Mbps, 8-bit, or 720p, H.264, MP4, 2Mbps, 8-bit
- Instagram: 1080p or 720p, H.264, MP4, 3.5Mbps, 8-bit

3. Live video transmission

Let's now look at how we transmit video information from one point to another. There are two major families of formats to do this, deterministic and probabilistic.

3.1 Deterministic Video

In traditional live video formats like *Serial Digital Interface*[17] (SDI for short) or *HDMI* in the home, image and video are sent through a cable in a predetermined, sequential fashion. There is no uncertainty about the order of frames, nor any room for a change in parameters once the connection is established. It is what is called a *deterministic*, or *synchronous*, flow.

The definition of deterministic is a *"system in which no randomness is involved in the development of future states. A deterministic model will always produce the same output from a given starting condition or initial state"*[18].

Feeding video in a deterministic fashion has several advantages. For one, the result is quasi-instantaneous, and even more importantly, entirely predictable in its transit time. There is no buffering involved in frame retransmission. Another advantage of using deterministic workflows is that they are quite simple to configure; they operate on a "plug-and-play" principle. Finally, they are very robust. Unless you unplug the connector, video will flow from one output to the next input.

The format is not perfect, though. One of the drawbacks of using deterministic video workflows is that the distance between emitter and receiver is limited in several implementations. If the signal gets degraded because of a long distance, it will stop working.

---

[17] See https://en.wikipedia.org/wiki/Serial_digital_interface
[18] See https://en.wikipedia.org/wiki/Deterministic_system

For HD SDI, for example, signal will be lost after approximately 275 feet / 80 meters, unless the signal is boosted with an amplifier. HDMI is even more restrictive, at 50 feet / 15 meters. This can be countered by converting the cable to an optical fiber, for example.

Since each output corresponds to a specific input, it is also difficult to scale up. Devices that work on multiple videos need a lot of inputs and outputs, plus a ton of cable and switching capabilities (fig. 27).

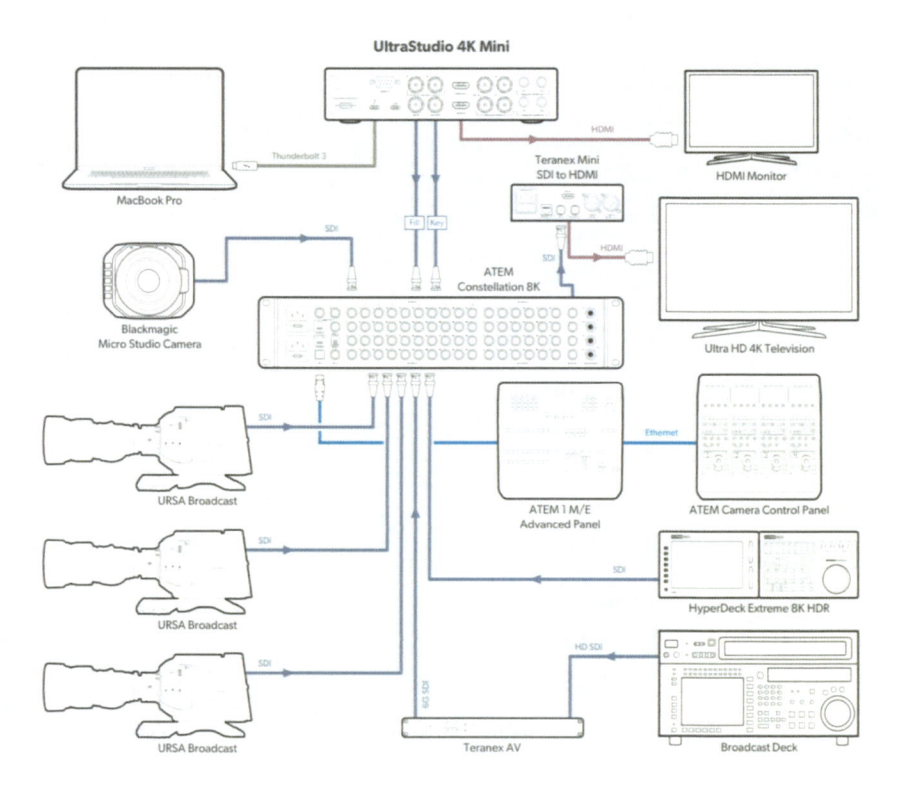

Figure 27 - Deterministic SDI system for live production by Blackmagic.

This means that deterministic video production workflows tend to require a lot of hardware, cable, and setup time. Their robustness is unmatched, but they lack in flexibility leading, for broadcasters, to large and expensive production infrastructures that are not always 100% booked.

Typical deterministic workflows include:

- Traditional television studios (SDI)
- Sporting events (SDI)
- Mobile studios (OB, or *Outside Broadcast* trucks in SDI)
- Home video (HDMI)

When there arises a need to cover long distances, deterministic workflows can become very expensive. For example, to re-broadcast a major event from one continent to another, the signal needs to be managed with a dedicated and protected mechanism (dedicated optical fiber, commonly called *dark fiber*, for example) that maintains signal integrity. This can cost a lot of money, so access to those technologies is restricted to a few major players.

In the last few years, another type of live video transmission principle has arisen: *Probabilistic*. It makes live streaming much more affordable and has democratized the access to live audiences for millions of content creators worldwide.

3.2 Probabilistic workflows

Probabilistic (also known as *asynchronous*) workflows assume that the sender does not control the chain of transmission to the receiver. This means that there is no way to ensure that the information will reach the receiver in the right order, at the right time or even reach it at all. This is the case, for example, when information transits through the public internet (fig. 28) or a *Wide Area Network* (WAN).

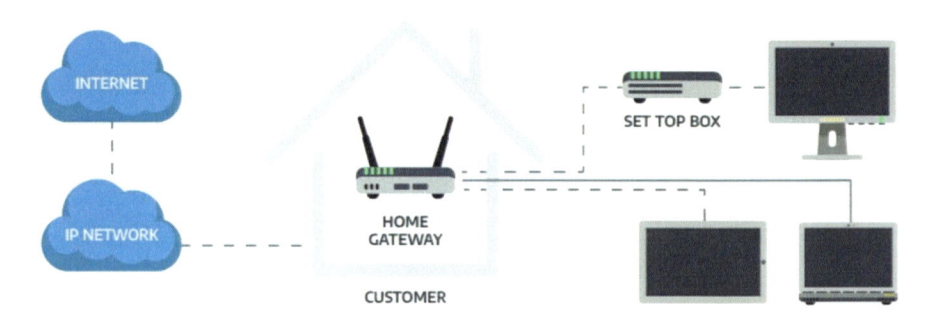

Figure 28 - Example of a probabilistic workflow - IP based television

Probabilistic systems are based on the idea that you cannot be certain about results or future events, but you can judge whether they are likely, and act based on this judgment.

This means that, although the transmission of information is unreliable (contrary to deterministic methods), it is possible to plan accordingly and develop strategies to address those shortcomings.

But why would anyone go through all this trouble when deterministic workflows are available? Because of a variety of reasons:

- Probabilistic workflows are not limited in distance. Since they integrate and manage information loss, delays, and asynchronous transmission, they can use the public internet and cover any region of the world connected to the web.

- Each resource in a probabilistic network of resources can be addressed by any other resource, making the devices much more versatile and providing higher utilization.
- They are generally much cheaper to operate than deterministic workflows when covering multiple remote sites, as no private dedicated connection is required.
- The footprint for those workflows is generally smaller, as most devices can be connected to the network of resources with only one or two connectors.

Naturally, the fact that these workflows use probabilistic networks presents a few other disadvantages, such as latency and potential issues with *Quality of Service* (QoS), which can manifest itself as a loss in resolution, visible glitches and sometimes loss of signal.

To understand why QoS can be an issue, let's look at how deterministic systems consider the fact that bits of information do not travel sequentially through a single point to point path. We will look at the concept of *packets*, timing, and error correction, albeit at a high level (this is not a detailed guide to IP video, a subject that could be a very large book by itself).

3.2.1 Packets

Instead of sending one, continuous flow of information from point a to point b, probabilistic systems break down video into small chunks called *packets*. Then, figuratively, it pushes those packets in the other while a receiver, somewhere, awaits to receive those packets of information.

Since no two packets are guaranteed to take the same route from point a to point b, there is no assurance that the packets will arrive at the proper time, nor in the right order. Therefore, it is essential to do a few things:

First, we need to identify the packets, so the receiver can understand what it is receiving. Secondly, we need to time-stamp those packets, so the receiver knows in which order they should be re-assembled to present the video in the correct sequence. Thirdly, we need to understand how much time it takes for packets to reach point b, to allow sufficient buffer time so there is no loss of signal due to the receiver waiting for packets to arrive. Finally, we need a feedback mechanism to let the emitter know if some packets get lost on the way or corrupted, to give it a chance to re-transmit those packets. Let's now look at the mechanisms that were put in place to ensure that each of those problems are solved.

3.2.1.1 Packet timing

Knowing the time at which a packet was sent and received enables the system to understand the statistical distribution of latency. In other words, the system can know how long is the longest transit time for packets from A to B and plan a buffering strategy to ensure that once video starts streaming at destination, it is not interrupted due to missing packets.

There are two main technologies used to time packets. The first one is called *PTP*, or *Precision Time Protocol*. PTP works by continuously sending time, measuring the round-trip time between the sender and the receiver which are both "clocked" to this precision time source (fig 30). ST.2110, a protocol developed to allow the use of generic IP networks to transmit media (media over IP), uses PTP as its main timing methodology.

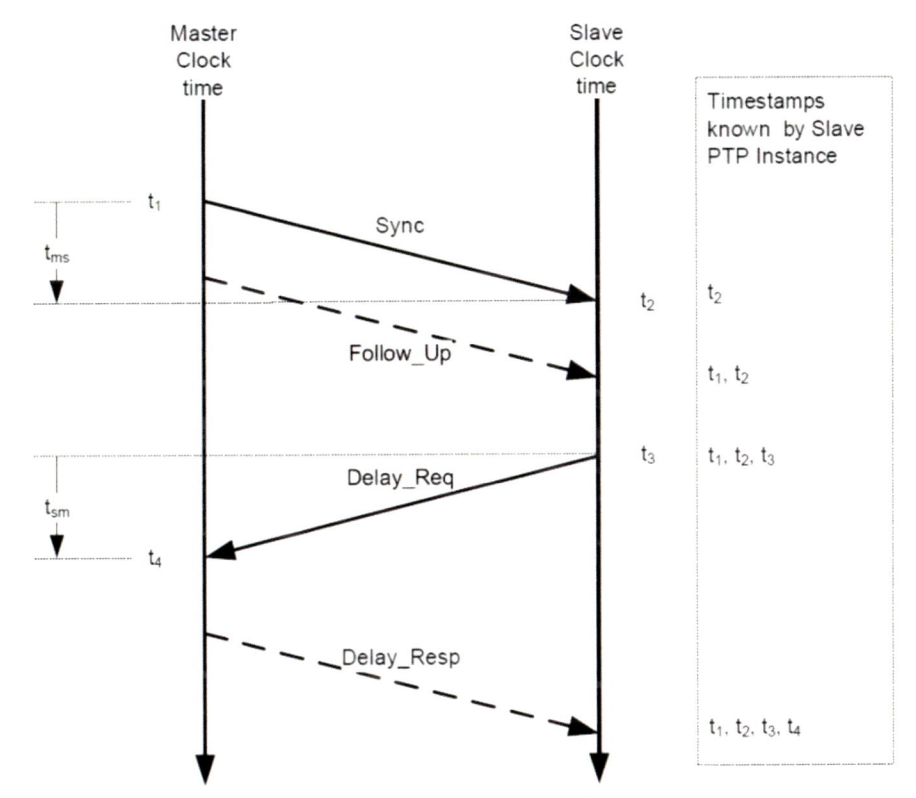

Figure 30 - Precision Time Protocol

Another mechanism used in IP video is *Network Time Protocol*[19] (NTP), the same protocol used by your computer, phone, and other connected devices to tell you what time it is without manual intervention.

NTP works through a network of government, public and volunteer systems that allow servers to transmit time. The source is an atomic clock, and depending how close the server is to this clock, there will be varying levels of precision to NTP (fig. 30).

---

[19] See https://en.wikipedia.org/wiki/Network_Time_Protocol

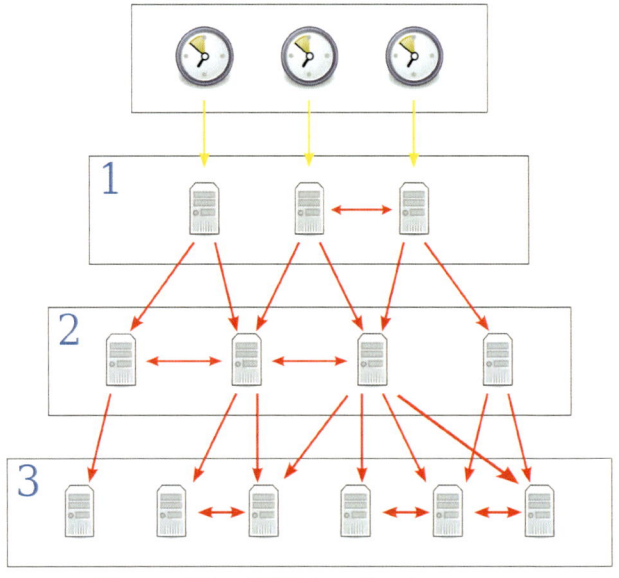

Figure 30 - NTP levels of servers

This strategy is used by IP streaming protocols like *Secure, Reliable Transport* (SRT), an open-source protocol developed by Haivision.

3.2.1.2 Error Prevention and Correction

Without going into too much detail, there are several mechanisms in place within Video over IP protocols to ensure that a video stream goes uninterrupted, even when packets get lost, corrupted or take too long to get to the receiver. The most well-known of those are *Forward Error Correction* (FEC), *Automatic Repeat reQuest* (ARQ) and *hitless fail-over*.

The principle behind FEC is that the system, duplicates some of the payload so some packets are sent multiple times across the network, reducing the chance that no copy of a packet reaches the receiver.

ARQ is *"an error control and packet recovery method for data transmission in which the receiver sends an alert to the sender if a packet is missing, so that the sender can resend the missing packet"*[20]. It is found in the SRT protocol developed by Haivision.

Hitless fail-over is a mechanism by which network switches route the packets through multiple paths. This prevents interruption of service when one of the switches is down, for example.

Error prevention and correction is not free, however. There is always a cost associated with the level of resilience of packet transmission in a probabilistic system, which can take the form of additional bandwidth, latency, or both.

3.2.2 Packet-based Video-over-IP protocols

As of the publication of this book, here are the most popular packet-based protocols that can be found in the video industry:

ST.2110
- Open source through SMPTE. Can be implemented in shared IP networks as well as internal dedicated networks (bringing its latency close to zero)

HTTP Live Streaming (HLS):
- Apple proprietary

MPEG-DASH:
- Open Source

Real-Time Messaging Protocol (RTMP):
- Open Source

Secure, Reliable Transport (SRT):
- Open Source, developed by Haivision

---

[20] See https://www.haivision.com/glossary/arq/

WebRTC (web-based, Real Time Communication):
- Free and open source

3.2.3 Which protocol is right for the job?

When discussing streaming protocols, just like codecs, there is no ideal, "one size fits all" approach that satisfies all production needs. In the case of protocols, a compromise is required between resilience and latency (fig. 31).

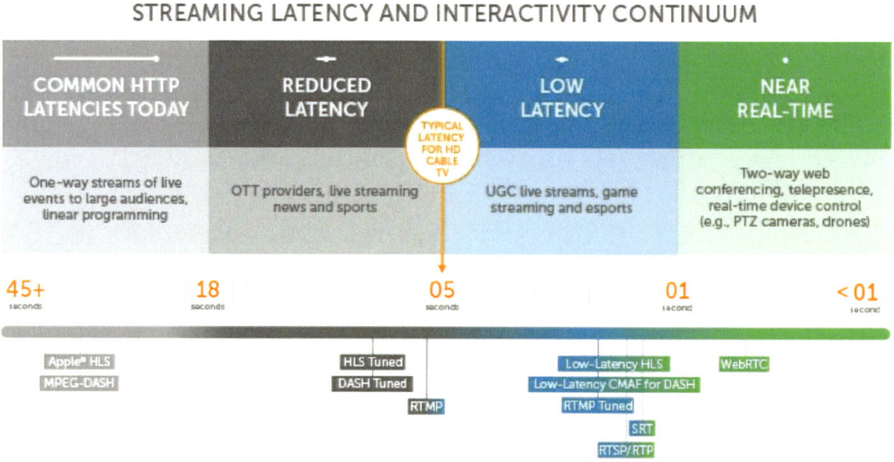

Figure 31 - Latency Vs. Streaming protocols (source: https://www.wowza.com/blog/streaming-protocols)

Low latency protocols like *WebRTC*, for example, strip the stream of all error-correcting features that add latency. This provides almost real-time delivery, which is required in applications where communication and immediacy of action is required. A very good example of this is with virtualized remote-control rooms, where there must not be any lag between a remote operator's editing decision and their execution in the cloud engine. Another example would be a betting site with real-time bets. That kind of site cannot allow a lag between a goal being scored and the betting decision, for obvious reasons.

The downside of near real-time streaming protocols is that a very fast and robust internet connection is required, as any delay in transmission will interrupt the stream.

At the opposite side of the spectrum, we find protocols that are not real-time, but show very strong robustness. Those are better suited to video on demand applications, which are not live by nature. For the viewer, preventing a loss of connection and program interruption due to buffering is paramount, and mechanisms like adaptive bitrate (e.g. lowering bitrate if a poor internet connection is detected) and error correction (preventing loss of frames) ensure the story is not going to get interrupted while watching.

ST.2110 could be put in a category of its own, as it can be almost instantaneous when used in a managed, dedicated infrastructure, but can also be used in shared IP infrastructures, with the associated "cost" in latency.

4. Image Capture Fundamentals

So far, we have covered most of the important aspects of compression and transport for video, whether file-based or live streaming. While this book is aimed at technical folks in the industry, I strongly believe that to ensure a long and successful career, it is important that "techies" understand what goes on in front of the camera.

We will therefore look at the technical and creative challenges in capturing the image itself, and the kind of compromises that film crews must address to:

a) Tell a compelling story
b) Provide maximum creative latitude in post-production to
c) Make the final image as beautiful as possible

4.1 Cinematography - what goes into an image

In previous chapters, we focused on the container. While this is the essence of our technical work behind the camera, it is refreshing to also understand the *contents* of the frame. During production, the main image specialist is the *Director of Photography*, abbreviated DP or DoP depending on whether you work in Canada, the US, in Europe or elsewhere.

The DoP is in charge of making sure every image meets the technical specifications of the camera used in production, as well as translating creative intent from the director into technical elements to support the story. In a nutshell, here are the technical elements that comprise the image inside the container (fig. 32):

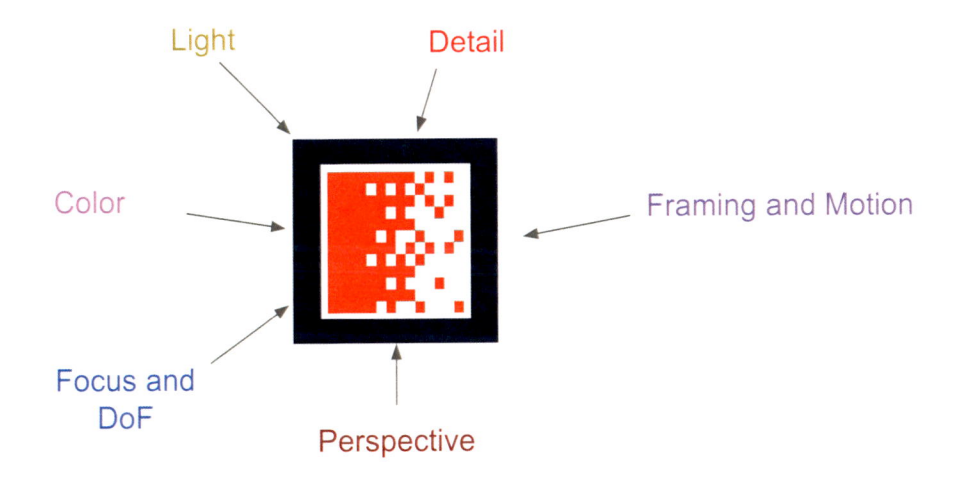

Figure 32 - Technical elements inside a frame of video

The DoP must ensure optimal conditions in the form of:

a) Lighting on set, and how it will translate on the sensor.
b) color, including proper filtering to ensure color integrity.
c) focus and Depth of Field (DoF) so the viewer looks at the right things on the screen.
d) perspective, which conveys a subtle emotion.
e) detail, so the main elements clearly visible, and
f) framing and motion, to convey the right message depending on the story.

The following sections will help you better understand each of those aspects, their inter-relationships and how they affect the technical work downstream.

4.2 Lighting and its effect on image capture

Each camera generation has a sensor that will be more or less sensitive to light; as a rule of thumb, sensors increase the capability of delivering clear images at lower light levels with each new generation.

The capability of a sensor to convert light particles (photons) to an electrical charge (electrons) is called *Quantum Efficiency*. With current quantum efficiency above 98% on modern cameras, it is not realistic to expect significant gains in terms of maximum light intensity reaching the sensor. What manufacturers focus on instead is eliminating noise in low light, which is where they can increase a camera's overall *latitude*.

In an environment where the lighting is controlled (e.g. studio, sound stage, etc.), the DoP will create a lighting environment that allows lens aperture to match the desired Depth of Field (see section 4.4) while capturing interesting highlights, steering viewer attention, and setting overall mood with multiple lighting fixtures, much like painters of old would do in their portraits.

In an environment where lighting is not generated (e.g. outdoors), the DoP will use filters to control the amount of incoming light and, if possible, light diffusing and focusing devices like bounces, silks and other tools found in the *grip*'s arsenal. The grip department's role in lighting is to provide and install lighting and light controlling fixtures that meet the DoP's prescriptions to achieve the Director's intent on a shot safely and efficiently.

For those interested in learning more about this fascinating art, there are several excellent references written by very competent authors[21].

4.3 Color integrity

As we've discussed before, the second property of light, after intensity, is color. A camera's capability is judged very critically on its latitude for intensity, but for color it is judged on its capability to reproduce a scene accurately in terms of colorimetry.

---

[21] For example: Cinematography - Theory and Practice by Blain Brown

Our visual system (combination of eyes, optic nerve, and visual cortex) is quite tolerant and easily adjusts its perception of color based on varying sources of light. For example, we do not perceive a Caucasian skin as yellow when lit by candlelight.

For a digital camera, however, this is EXACTLY the way it will record light, as its input is related to the *illuminant* of the scene. A scene lit by incandescent light will look yellow, the same scene lit by a neon will appear green, and daylight will look blue, due to the spectral diffusion of those sources of light (fig. 33), which creates peaks of intensity.

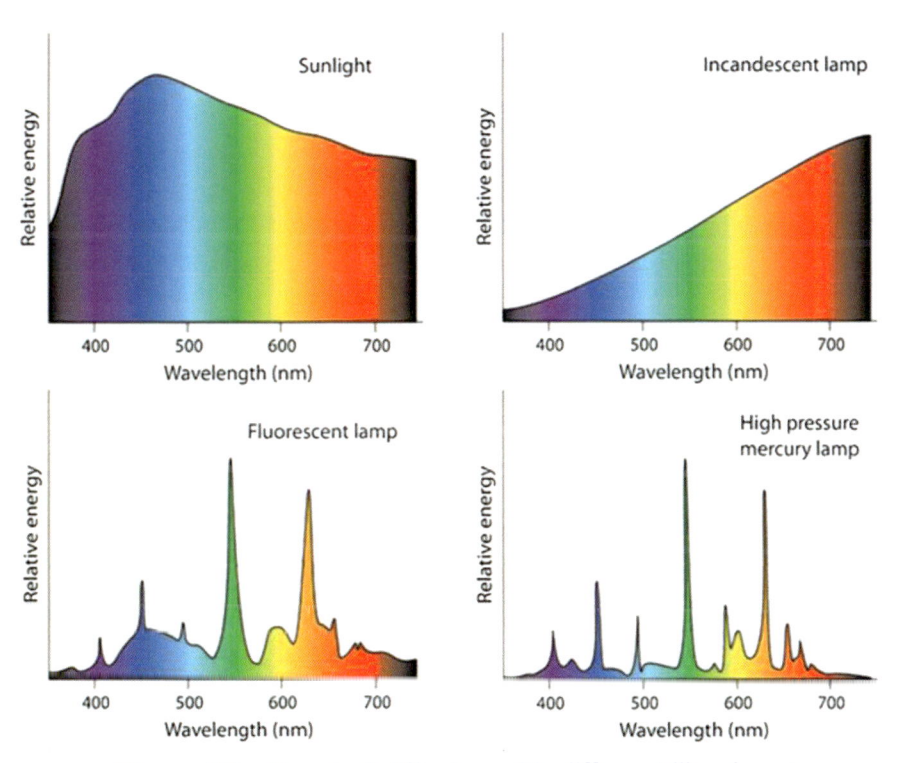

Figure 33 - Spectral diffusion with different illuminants

To make the scene look identical in different sources, cameras are equipped with a *White Balance* mechanism, which applies a transformation to make the image look proper on a specific display. For example, applying a tungsten white balance to a scene lit that way on a television camera will make the white look proper on a D65 *color temperature* video screen. For more information on light, its properties and color science, you can refer to our other guide on *High Dynamic Range*[22].

After applying the proper white balance, the color gamut needs to look natural and reflect accurately what was in front of the camera. If white balance has been applied but skin tones and certain colors do not look right, it may be caused by one of the following factors:

- Infrared pollution, which gives a reddish-brownish look to dark elements in the image (fig. 34) - solved with an infrared filter.

- Partial-spectrum sources of lighting, like some consumer-grade LED light sources, for example, which do not represent the entire color spectrum.

- Mixed sources of light, like filming a scene where light comes from outside, a neon and a candlelight in the scene, for example. This is solved by settling on a single-color temperature, by filtering the windows and removing neon lighting, for example.

---

[22] HDR for Television and Motion Pictures: A Digital Troublemaker Guide. Available on Amazon.

Figure 34 - Filtered image without (top) and with an IR filter (bottom) - source: https://www.filmmakersacademy.com/rod-dragon-ir-filtration/

4.4 Focus and Depth of Field

Focus is an important feature filmmakers use to direct the viewer's attention in the frame. The limits in the scene where people and things appear to be in focus are called the *depth of field*, and this depth is expressed in linear distance to the camera, from near to far focus.

Depending on several factors, depth of field will be narrow, sometimes only a few centimeters deep, up to being so wide as nearing infinity. The main factors influencing depth of field are the distance to focus, the *aperture* (or iris) and the factor of *magnification* (i.e. how close or far from the subject of interest we are).

There are several tools available to calculate depth of field based on those factors, like the much-appreciated *pCAM* app on the Apple iPhone. In general terms, the casual reader can make the following assumptions about depth of field:

- Larger sensors require the camera to be closer or the focal length to be higher (i.e. "zoomed in") to provide the same framing as a smaller sensor, thus increasing the magnification factor and reducing the DoF significantly.
- Darker scenes require a wider aperture, which drastically reduces DoF.
- To achieve deep DoF, television cameras use smaller sensors (typically ⅔ in. 3-chip sensors) than cinema cameras.
- Large sensors are a challenge to use in television due to the limited DoF when framed to typical TV values.

4.5 Focal Length and Perspective

The Focal Length of a lens dictates how close or far objects and people will appear in a scene. When we are working with fixed focal length lenses, those are called *prime lenses*. Lens systems with variable focal length are called *zoom lenses*.

The smallest focal lengths show a very wide field of view. At one end of the spectrum, we have *fish-eye* lenses, which can be found on most smartphones and door peepholes. These lenses will distort the visual field, making facial features look almost comical when close to the camera. They are seldom used for anything closer than a very wide shot, except when the filmmaker is trying to convey a sense of insanity, or confusion in the talent on-screen. That can be observed in original Star Trek episodes, for example, when crew members and sometimes the Captain himself are struck with temporary insanity.

In the medium range of focal length, you will find a field of view that approximates human vision. Those lenses are typically used for medium to wide shots, to give a proper sense of scale to a scene.

Very long focal lengths are called *telephoto* for prime lenses. Those possess immense scaling properties, bringing distant backgrounds closer to the camera and flattening facial features while providing a narrow depth of field. Those are typically used for close-ups, as they are the most flattering to talent on screen. So-called "beauty" and "hero" shots use the telephoto lens systematically.

4.6 Detail in Video

In a video frame, detail is expressed as the capacity to perceive changes in contrast, which indicate the edge of objects as well as their texture. It is the resulting quality of the clarity of image elements due to a combination of several factors:
- Depth of field and focus (i.e. whether detail is visible or blurry)
- Lighting (does it provide enough contrast to perceive edges and textures)
- Shutter speed and motion (are the images still enough to appear clearly or are they blurred due to movement)

It could be argued that one of the most important roles of the cinematographer is to ensure there is detail in the frame where the director wants to focus the action, and that several compromises need to be made to achieve this level of detail while maintaining other important characteristics of the image (e.g. motion, perspective, etc.).

4.7 Framing and Motion

In general terms, filmmaking conventions dictate that framing and motion are dependent on a continuum between action and emotion. As a rule of thumb, scenes where the filmmaker wants to convey a sense of action are going to include a lot of motion and will be shot wide with shorter focal lengths, which allow the viewer to perceive the motion and enjoy a deep focus to appreciate all the levels of action.

When the scene needs to convey emotion, the motion is typically going to be minimal, usually imperceptible to the viewer, and the focal lengths are going to be quite long. Framing is going to be tight on the facial features of the on-screen talent, and the face is usually the only thing in clear focus. This immerses the audience in the actor's performance and typically elicits an emotional response, especially when accompanied by evocative music (sound being a subject worth several books on its own).

4.8 The role of image technicians and engineers with regards to Image Capture

Newcomers to the industry, especially in non-creative trades, should refrain from making "creative" or "editorial" calls when working on a production, as it is widely panned and will reflect poorly on the individual making those comments, even if he or she thinks it's warranted. Filmmaking is a team effort, and each member in this team has a specific responsibility.

The responsibility of image engineers and technicians is to bring technical issues to the attention of their supervisor. What happens then is not their responsibility. The weight of making a compelling piece of art that will please audiences is the burden of creatives, and they have the final word on how to shoot their work.

To better expand on the point above, section 5 of this book identifies the types of technical issues that are typically within the realm of imaging technicians and engineers, and briefly details what usually causes them and how to identify them.

5. Video Quality Control

This section is meant to be a peek in the field of video *Quality Control*, or QC. There is much, much more to Video QC than what is described below, but it should be sufficient to give a sense of what can go wrong, technically, and why those issues occur.

5.1 Spatial resolution issues

These technical issues are related to the perception of detail in each frame from a video image sequence. Issues that deal with the playback of the sequence are detailed in the following section, which talks about *temporal resolution*.

5.1.1 Out of focus

When a shot is not focusing on the subject of interest. Typically, due to wide iris, improper focus distance on the lens, wide sensor used with long focal length, or a combination of these. Once again, the role of the technical crew is to note the focus issue, not to make editorial comments on it.

5.1.1.1 Peaking Monitor
A peaking monitor is the main tool used in production to ensure elements in the shot are in focus. There are two ways to monitor peaking. In the first method, each block of pixels where there is high contrast, denoting clear edges and textures that are in focus, is represented with a red overlay. To see those areas clearly, the image is shown in a monochromatic fashion.

Another method for monitoring peaking is to add electronic edge enhancement to the image, creating an exaggeratedly high contrast, helping determine where focus is by looking at the edge of features on the screen.

5.1.2 Aliasing

Aliasing, or the apparition of spatial artifacts that were not present in front of the camera, is often caused by scene detail that is finer than the resolution of the sensor capturing the image, thus creating weird artifacts when detail is shifting from one pixel to another. This is the main reason why talent on screen avoids wearing pinstripe patterns, for example.

In more recent times, aliasing often occurs with very high-resolution screens on set, for example an Ultra HD screen filmed with an HD camera or delivered in HD, as can be seen in several concert videos.

5.2 Temporal resolution issues

These issues are not present when looking at frames individually but will be noticeable when playing the video at normal speed.

5.2.1 Judder

Judder is a perceptible motion artifact which, in layman's terms, makes the video look "not fluid". It typically occurs when inconsistent frame rates and shutter speeds are used, for example shooting at 24 fps for video delivery at 60 fps with a 1/48s shutter. Normally, to avoid judder, delivery frame rates and shutter speeds should be multiples of capture (e.g. 30 fps capture for 60 fps presentation).

Once again, It Is possible that judder is introduced voluntarily by the creatives, in order, for example, to provide a sense of confusion to the viewer, so it should be reported without creative commentary.

5.2.2 Excessive motion blur

Excessive motion blur typically occurs with low frame rate and low shutter speed capture, when there is a lot of motion in the image, what is called *optical flow* (net motion on the sensor due to motion from the scene and the camera).

5.3 Color and light resolution issues

In this section we will discuss the most frequent issues encountered with light and color management detected in post-production.

5.3.1 Out of gamut

Each project is running in a certain color space with a defined transfer function. For example, for HDTV, the color space is BT.709 and the transfer function is Gamma 2.4.

It may happen that some shots, or the post-production workflow, are saturated outside the delivery color gamut. Video technicians use a tool called the *Vectorscope* to monitor the color gamut and ensure it stays within the given boundaries of the project, typically BT.709 (SDR), DCI P3 (DCinema) or BT.2020 (HDR).

It is also possible that color space conversion was performed (or not, or incorrectly) during post-production; in that case, colors will appear to be off, like, for example, using a DCinema source in video without applying the proper color space transform.

5.3.2 Clipping

Clipping is the technical issue related to the fact that the sensor was filled with electrons during integration time (e.g. shutter speed), and detail was lost. In traditional photography and film, this is called overexposure. Lost detail due to clipping is often unrecoverable.

5.3.3 Dark noise

Dark noise occurs when there is not enough light hitting the sensor, either because the scene was too dark, the lens aperture too small, or both. The phenomenon is caused by a low signal (light we want to capture) to noise (spontaneous electrons not caused by light) ratio.

5.3.4 Skin tones and color rendition

Improper color rendition can be caused by multiple factors, including, but not limited to, infrared pollution, mixed lighting sources, use of strong filters and low-quality light sources (e.g. consumer-grade LED). Such problematic shots are challenging to fix because of an uneven illumination, meaning that color balance will fix some colors, but not others (i.e. you cannot correct a color that is not there in the first place).

5.3.5 Color temperature

On film cameras shooting RAW, color temperature can easily be set in post-production using references on screen (which is why shooting reference charts when a new lighting setup is installed is a good idea). For many types of cameras, however, color temperature is burnt into the image. Improper white balance will lead to shots where white will look yellow, green, blue, or somewhere in between, depending on the illuminant, which can be corrected if said camera has sufficient bit depth at capture, otherwise proper color correction may not be possible.

5.3.6 Light and Color QC tools

Here is an overview of some of the tools available in the technician's arsenal to help objectively validate that the image conforms to specifications from a color and luminance standpoint.

5.3.6.1 Waveform Monitor

The modern *Waveform Monitor* is a digital emulation of the original, analog display of line voltage on an oscilloscope. Hence, what it shows is luminance level on the vertical axis (corresponding to voltage in the days of tube tv) and position in the image from left to right (corresponding to the scan line of video).

If we had a single line of video, it would look like an x-y graph, but since we're analyzing a progressive frame, it shows luminance for all pixels, from left to right. It does not indicate where those pixels are vertically in the image,[23] but it ensures we do not have pixels beyond the thresholds of clipping and dark noise.

As we are free from analog constraints, there are multiple display variations for waveform. The vertical axis, for example, can be expressed in code values, percentage of code values, or even display luminance for transfer functions like Gamma, HLG and PQ (fig. 35-36).

Figure 35 - Sample image for Waveform

---

[23] Some advanced waveform monitors offer a line select function which helps diagnose the problematic vertical area(s) in the image, but this is usually not found in software-based monitors nor entry level hardware.

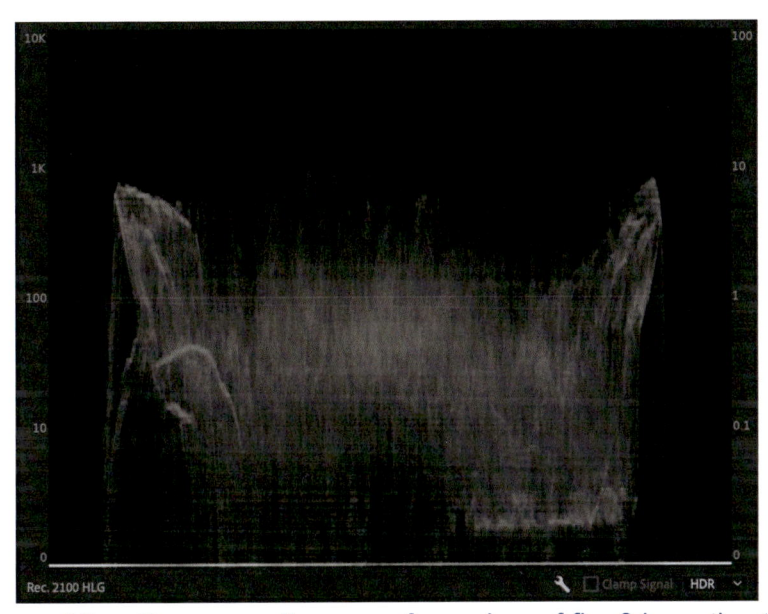

Figure 36a - Corresponding waveform view of fig. 34 - notice the vertical axis in display-referred *nits* (left) and % of code value (right)

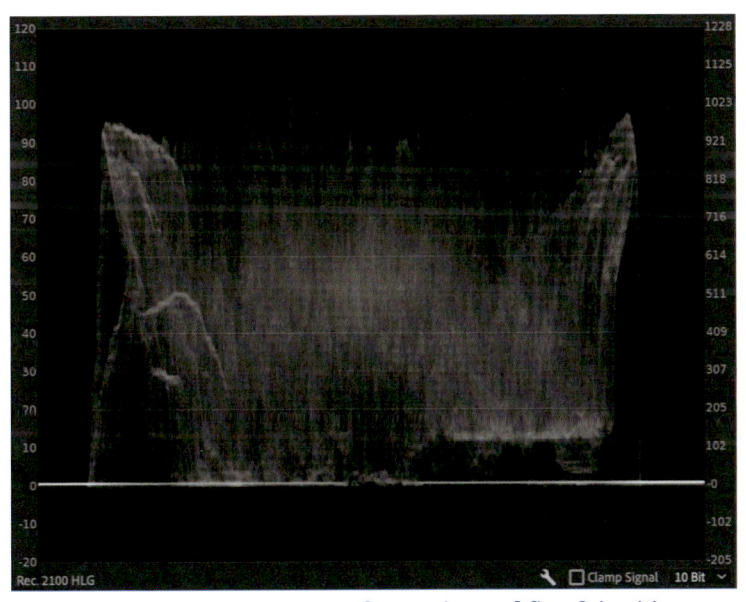

Figure 36b - Corresponding waveform view of fig. 34 with percentage on the vertical left axis and Code Values on the vertical right axis (in this case, 10-bit, or CV 0-1023)

5.3.6.2 Vectorscope

The *Vectorscope* is another digital descendent of analog tools. "The vectorscope's *graticule* roughly represents saturation as distance from the center of the circle, and hue as the angle, in standard position, around it"[24], as can be seen in figure 37.

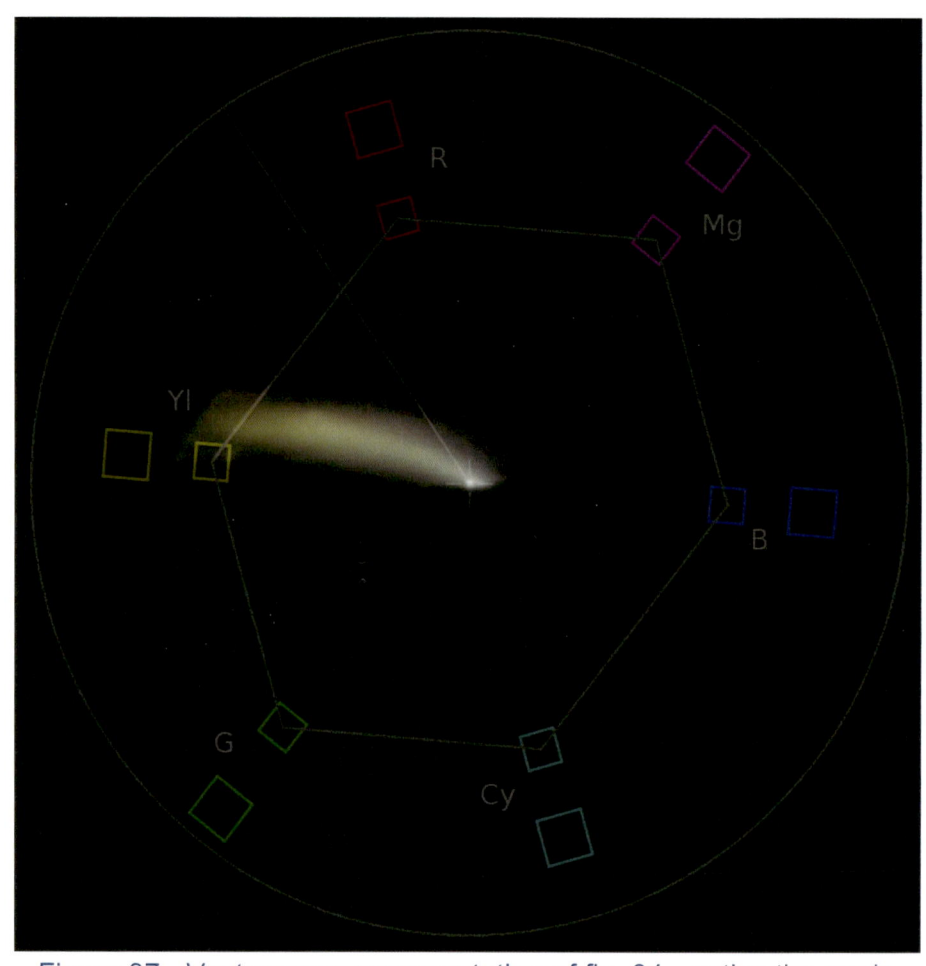

Figure 37 - Vectorscope representation of fig. 34 - notice the angle representing a yellow-red hue and the spread from the center highlighting a high degree of saturation in that hue.

---

[24] See https://en.wikipedia.org/wiki/Vectorscope for additional details

5.3.6.3 Histogram

The Histogram is a digital representation of image luminance, similar but different from the waveform (which takes its roots in analog signal monitoring).

It represents the number of pixels at each level of luminance in the image, typically on a horizontal axis although some vendors propose a vertical version as well (fig. 38).

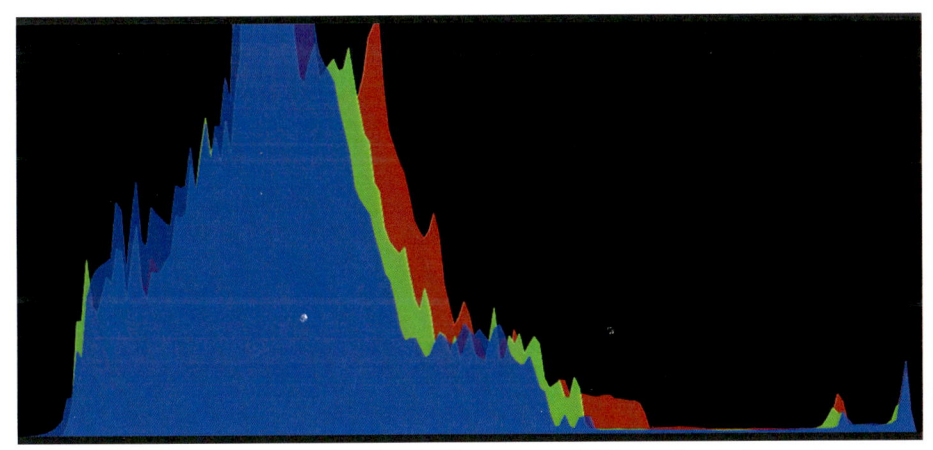

Figure 38 - Histogram for Red, Green, and Blue pixels in an image. The graph indicates the percentage of pixels (vertical axis) at each level of light intensity (horizontal axis), from dark noise (extreme left) to clipping (extreme right).

5.3.6.4 False Color (also called Heat Map)

False color was created to help filmmakers identify the exact area in an image where too much or not enough light is present. Unlike waveform and histograms, it superimposes the level of luminance on the x-y plane of the image in the form of color gradients. Although there are variations between manufacturers, the colors typically alter from "cold" colors (green blue purple) where the image is below ideal exposure levels to grayscale and green at nominal exposure levels, then shifting to "warm" colors (yellow orange red) where the image is nearing clipping (fig. 39).

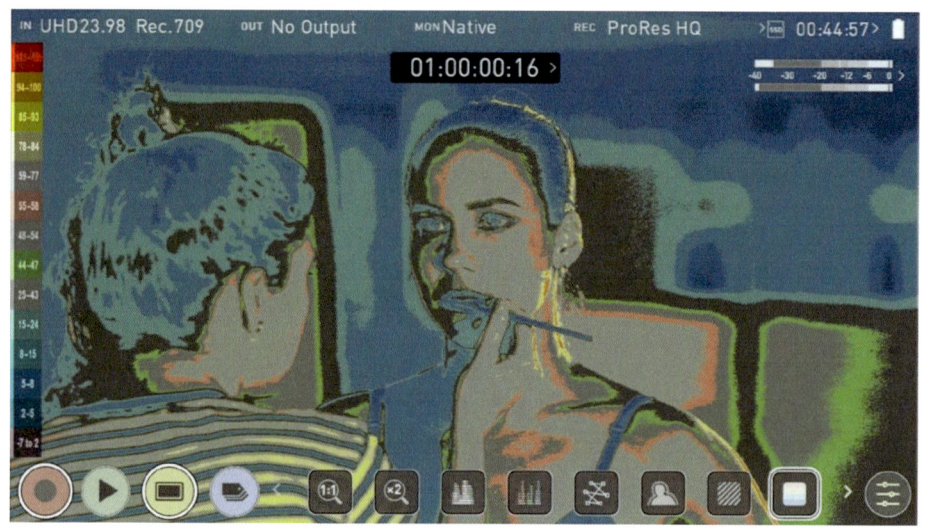

Figure 39 - False Color as implemented by manufacturer Atomos on their field monitors (see https://support.atomos.com/hc/en-us/articles/5457641843855-Monitoring-Features-Focus-Peaking-Zebra-and-False-Color)

5.4 Compression issues

Compression issues are technical problems caused by improper digitizing of source assets, either during source quantizing or subsequent compression. Aggressive compression will leave visible *artifacts* on the image, which the imaging technician should report.

5.4.1 Banding

Banding, as we've discussed earlier in this book, occurs when the bit depth is lower than what the gradient in an image requires. Instead of a smooth transition, the viewer will perceive bands of color with clear boundaries. There are different possible avenues to correct banding issues. In the old days when bit depth was too limited, dithering was used as a technique to smooth out rough gradients. Modern solutions are typically to increase the bit depth of the project, or to modify the color to reduce the number of code values required to express the image. This process, when adapting theatrical or UHD content to HD, is sometimes called a "trim pass".

5.4.2 Macro blocks

Marco Blocks are visible square or rectangular patches on the image. They occur when the compression rate is very high, and the codec cannot compress the image effectively anymore, leaving visible artifacts instead of detail (fig. 40).

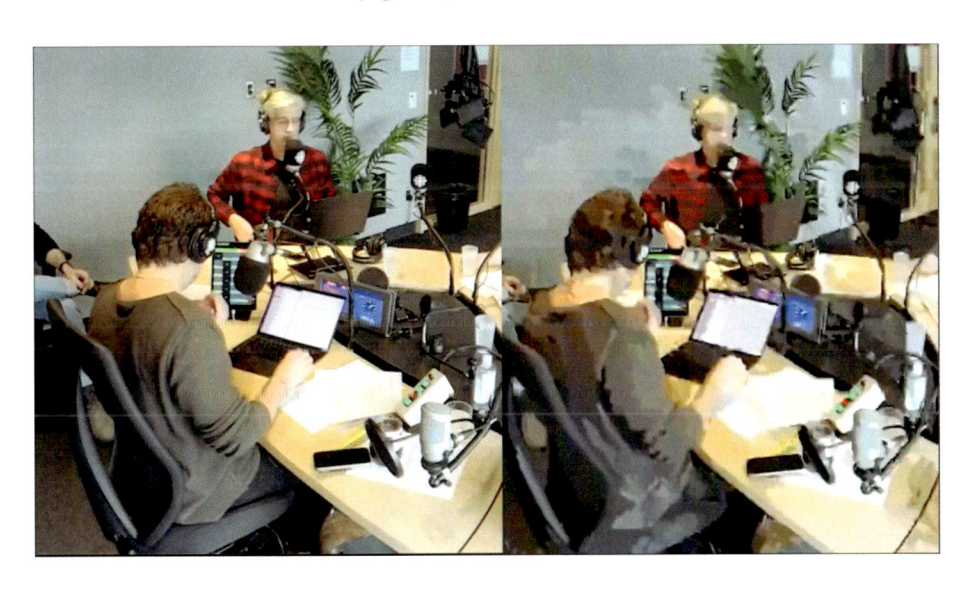

Figure 40 – Macro blocks due to high compression (right)

5.4.3 Corrupted frames

Corrupted frames will be obvious to even the casual observer. If the corrupted frame is an *I frame* within a *GOP*, it will corrupt the sequence until the next *I frame* is read.

5.5 Automatic quality control software

As it would be quite cumbersome to perform all these QC operations manually, several companies have developed software-based QC tools, verifying all the above-mentioned features plus several other more advanced ones.

As an example, Interra Systems' *Baton* Quality Control software performs roughly 100 tests on a video sequence and provides extensive reporting.

5.6 To learn more

The reader wishing to learn more about common quality issues is invited to follow the link below see hundreds of examples from the European Broadcasting Union: https://qc.ebu.io

6. Graphics Fundamentals

In this section, we will provide a brief glimpse into the world of graphics as applied to broadcast and motion pictures. There are two main families of graphics used in video: Vector-based, and Raster-based.

6.1 Vector Graphics

Vector graphics are graphics rendered by a computer using mathematical geometry formulae (e.g. lines, arcs, etc.). Vector images are therefore resolution independent and can be scaled at will without any loss in detail. The best example of vector-based graphics is typography. Fonts on your computer, for example, can be scaled without losing detail.

Another great advantage of vector graphics is that they take a very small amount of data to store, compared to raster graphics, and that amount of data is independent of the final resolution of the image.

The main downside of vector graphics is that creating photorealistic graphics is very complex when relying strictly on geometry.

Logos, scoreboards, lower third news tickers and end credits are typical uses of vector-based graphics in video.

6.1.1 HTML5 Vector graphic formats

Although there are several proprietary vector-based graphic systems and formats in the industry, there is growing popularity for a standardized, open-source normalization, which has translated into the HTML5 graphic APIs gaining more and more prominence.

The two main HTML5 graphics elements are *canvas*, which uses the code word <canvas> in JavaScript, and *Scalable Vector Graphics*, which uses the <svg> code word (fig. 41).

```html
<!DOCTYPE html>
<html>
<body>

<svg width="100" height="100">
  <circle cx="50" cy="50" r="40" stroke="green" stroke-width="4" fill="yellow" />
</svg>

</body>
</html>
```

Figure 41 - Example of SVG code representing a green-edged circle with a yellow fill

6.1.2 Overlaying vector-based graphics on video

Since the approach for vector-based graphics is to generate the image from code, it will automatically be overlaid to video without the need for any special process. This will not be the case for raster graphics, however, which will by default overlay the whole raster over the video. In the following section we will look at the different methods used to overlay raster graphics or images on video.

6.2 Raster Graphics

Raster graphics are an array of pixels which are pre-rendered in a specific resolution.

One of the main reasons for using raster graphics is to achieve photo-realistic resolution, which is very difficult to achieve using drawn, vector-based graphics. This comes at the expense of file size, though, as each single pixel in the raster needs to be provided a value. The larger the size of the raster, the larger the file size.

To highlight the difference between raster and vector-based graphics, let's consider a small circle (fig. 42). The circle, at a small resolution, is identical in both raster and vector versions.

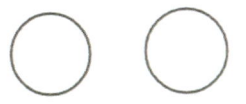

Figure 42 - Vector (left) versus raster (right) - small resolution

As the raster is made at a specific resolution, we cannot scale it the same way as the vector graphic; if we scale it up significantly, it will become "pixelated", showing its limited resolution (fig. 43).

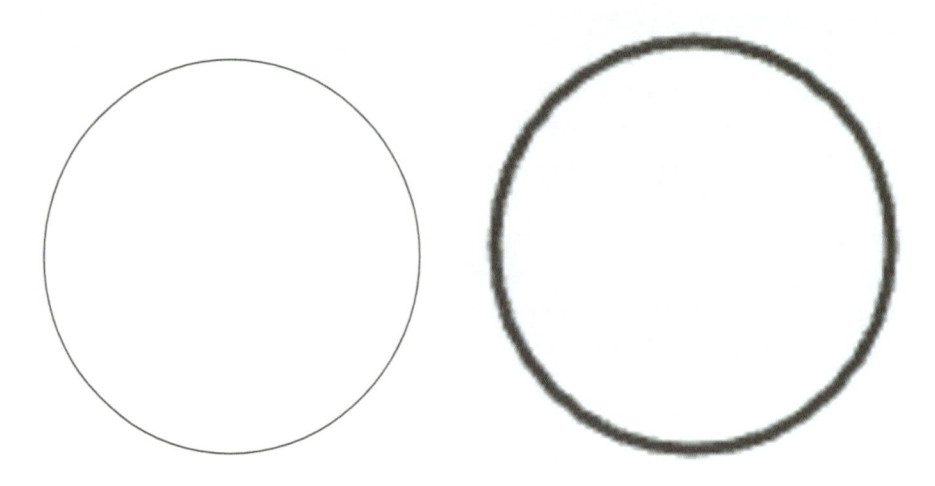

Figure 43 - Larger scale circle in vector (left) versus scaled-up raster (right) - notice the pixelation on the right due to the small raster size of the original graphic (fig. 41).

When creating raster-based graphics, it is therefore paramount that the graphics are created in the highest possible resolution that the video will ever use. For example, if the final product is to have an eventual UHD release but the graphics are designed in HD, those will need to be re-created or upscaled to fit the new resolution.

Overlaying raster graphics to an existing video is more complicated than with vector graphics, which are just drawn over the video track. When we want a shape, for example, to be overlaid without the background pixels, we need to assign a "transparency" value to those background pixels, otherwise they will be visible in the final composite.

6.2.1 Video transparency - raster graphics

In this section, we will look at the two different approaches to managing transparency in raster images: *keying* and *alpha matting*.

6.2.1.1 Keying

Modern raster graphic keying originates from the analog world. The principle is simple: a certain pixel value, whether hue, luminance, or a combination of both, is defined as the *key*. Any pixel within the raster that has the same value is interpreted as transparent and is removed from the raster during raster compositing over the video.

The most well-known keying colors are green and blue, which have traditionally been used in cinema and video and are often colloquially known as green-screen (fig. 44) and blue-screen.

Figure 44 - Green chroma keying for a weather map overlay

6.2.1.2 Alpha Matting

The downside of using a key is that the color is uniformly removed from the entire raster. What happens, for example, if a green key is used but the talent on screen wears a green piece of clothing, is that the piece of clothing will also become transparent.

Another issue is that lighting for a clean key is challenging. If the talent is too close to the background, for example, some of the green color will spill over the edge of hair and clothes and create some ugly halo effect around the character. One way to alleviate this is to provide a wider tolerance for the keying color, but doing so will make the edge of the talent transparent, thus cutting some of the hair or clothes, for example.

The way to avoid all these issues is to add a gray scale overlay to the raster graphic image; a fourth channel (red, green, and blue being the three other pixel channels), called *alpha*.

By convention, the level of transparency of each composite R-G-B-Alpha pixel will be 100% if the alpha pixel is black, 0% if the alpha pixel is white, and semi-transparent based on the gray scale level if in between black and white (fig. 45).

Figure 45 - Alpha channel (right) showing areas of transparency to be overlaid to the R-G-B channels (left).

Another convention in the graphics world is to represent transparency in an image with a checkerboard pattern of white and gray squares (fig. 44, left).

The alpha channel can be hand drawn (which is quite cumbersome), based on the *depth map* of a scene (using *lidar* or other tools to determine depth of pixels in relationship to the camera) or starting from a chroma key with further refinement applied by a visual effects artist.

6.2.2 Raster graphic formats

The most popular raster graphic formats are naturally those that have provisions to store alpha channel information to composite them onto video. For still images, those formats are *Portable Network Graphics* (PNG) and *Tag Image File Format* (TIFF). PNGs tend to be the most popular choice currently, and are accepted in most graphics software, web browsers, computers, and mobile OS.

For graphic video sequences, there are not too many choices available. The most popular format right now is Apple's *ProRES 4444 Alpha*, which is supported by most professional graphic software.

6.3 Compositing graphics - software

Now that we have our graphic files, we need to integrate them with our background video. This is done either in real time, or in post-production.

For real-time compositing, the reader can look at several solutions on the market by companies like *VizRT, Ross* and *Grass Valley,* that use *Graphics Processing Units,* or GPUs, which are dedicated hardware for video compositing and processing in real-time. These solutions are relatively expensive and used by major broadcasters for live events, especially in the fields of news and sports.

When real-time processing is not mandatory, there are a plethora of affordable solutions that allow artists to composite video and graphics together. Each of those would be worthy of a manual on its own. Mainly, there are three families of such software: Software for still images and low-count frame sequences such as Adobe's *Photoshop*, software for compositing effects over video shots like Adobe's *After Effects* and software to overlay graphics on a full video timeline encompassing multiple shots like the editorial software Adobe *Premiere* and Blackmagic's editing and grading solution *DaVinci Resolve*.

7. Display Fundamentals

As the whole purpose of everything we do in video is to present said video to our viewers, it is important to take the time to understand what are the different types of display technologies available to the market, and what are their respective strengths and weaknesses.

7.1 CRT

Cathode Ray Tube television is the grandfather of display technologies. Although discontinued for a few decades, there are still a lot of standards to this day that are based on its characteristics.

The most significant standards traced back to CRT are arguably BT.709, which describes the color volume of High-Definition television, and BT.2035, which describes the viewing environment for subjective evaluation of image quality (in other words, how to setup the screening room in a post-production environment).

BT.709 describes both the color primaries and the transfer function of HDTV. Interestingly, the R, G and B color primaries are based on the best reproduction available with phosphor on CRT back in the 1990s. Modern display technologies can reproduce much more vibrant colors, but since the standard was never updated, they are still limited to the BT.709 color gamut.

For light intensity, the BT.709 standard uses the *Gamma* power function, which emulates electron response in the tube of a CRT display. Once again, modern display devices emulate this as they do not behave in the same way.

It is only with the advent of High Dynamic Range and Wide Color Gamut imagery (BT.2100) that we finally go beyond the traditional color volume of 20th century CRTs.

As for BT.2035, it defines a viewing environment where the maximum light intensity is 100 cd/m², which is only a fraction of what modern displays can achieve. With the advent of HDR, BT.2100 has room for displays that max between 1000 and 10 000 cd/m².

7.2 LCD

Short for Liquid Crystal Display, LCD is one of the first so-called "flat screen" technologies to replace CRT. Its introduction was quite revolutionary, as it allowed displays to be much larger, thinner, and lighter than CRT, while consuming significantly less power.

The LCD display is using a combination of layers to generate both light intensity and color for each pixel (fig. 46).

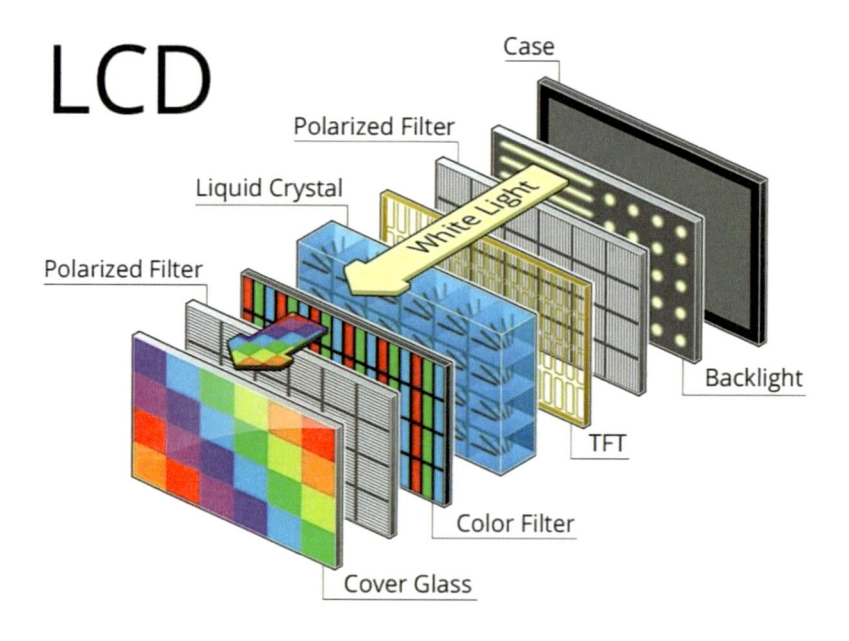

Figure 46 - LCD Panel. Source: https://www.eyecatchmedia.com/taxi-led-screen-or-lcd-screen-which-one-to-choose/

In the first layer in the back of the display, light is generated by a (typically) LED array, giving out the maximum light intensity available.

That light is then filtered through a polarizer to keep only linear polarized light (vertical filter in fig. 45). A combination of Thin Film Transistor (TFT) and liquid crystal cell array orient the liquid crystal in each cell depending on power applied to each cell. At full power, light is polarized 90 degrees, while idle does not orient the light.

Next, color filters provide color for each pixel, using Red, Green, and Blue sub-pixels.

Finally, a 90-degree polarizer (horizontal filter in fig. 45) filters out luminance depending on the power applied to each cell of liquid crystal, to provide final luminance for each pixel.

One of the main drawbacks of using LCD is that luminance is *subtracted* from the maximum luminance of the backlight. This has two major drawbacks: First, it consumes power unnecessarily for pixels that are not requiring it. Second, it lets some sliver of light through even at full power on the liquid crystal cells, which means that the blacks on screen will come out slightly gray.

More modern LCD displays are replacing the full backlight panel with an array of Light Emitting Diodes, which overall help increase contrast and reduce power consumption by providing more active luminance based on the video fed to the display.

7.3 QLED LCD

QLED stands for Quantum-Dot, Light Emitting Diode, Liquid Crystal Display (which is quite a mouthful!). It can be seen as an improvement over traditional LCD, by providing better color gamut than traditional sub-pixel color filters.

Instead of using basic while LED, the back panel utilizes narrower range blue LEDs, which then hit an enhancement layer of quantum dots (fig. 47).

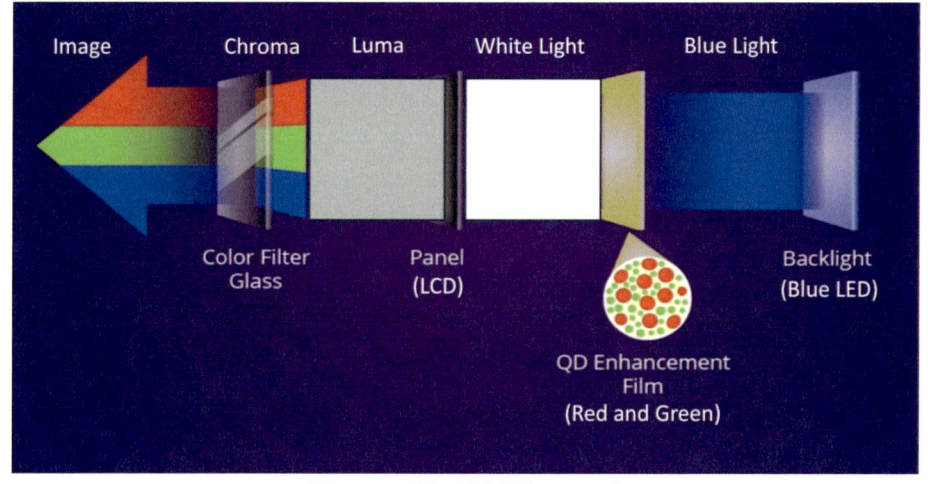

Figure 47 - QLED panel

Quantum dots are tiny particles that spontaneously generate light of a certain wavelength, which is proportional to the particle size. The enhancement layer has two sizes of quantum dots, emitting red and green light when hit by the blue LED.

By combining the blue LED with the green and red light emitted by the quantum dots, the display generates a brighter and narrower spectrum light than traditional LCD, which enables the display to generate much more vibrant and brighter colors than starting with a white LED back panel.

7.4 OLED

OLED stands for Organic, Light Emitting Diode. In a nutshell, it's an organic compound that spontaneously emits light when you apply current to it. It exists in three varieties: RGB, White and Quantum Dot Blue OLED.

The main advantage of OLED is that it is an emissive technology. If no current is applied to the compound, then no light is emitted. This is what allows OLED to provide much better contrast than competing technologies, by allowing the image to range from completely black to its peak luminance instead of trying to filter out light from a backlight.

7.4.1 RGB OLED

As the name suggests, RGB OLED consists of an array of pixels, each of which contains a red, green, and blue subpixel (fig. 48).

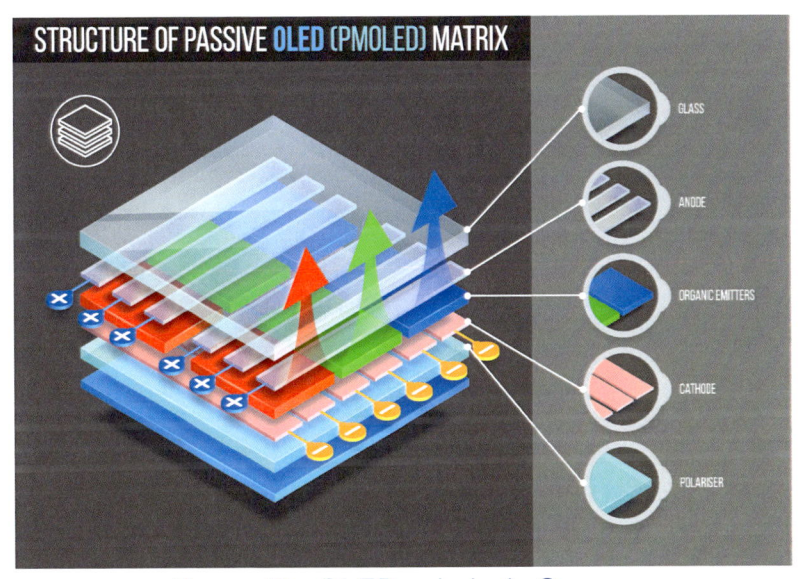

Figure 48 - OLED subpixel. Source: https://electronics360.globalspec.com/article/16130/fundamentals-of-oled-displays

On top of great contrast, RGB OLED achieves a very wide color gamut, providing rich natural colors. This all comes for a price, though. The main drawback of RGB OLED is easily its cost. It's extremely costly to manufacture, and exponentially depending on screen size due to low production yields. Other drawbacks include the risk of screen burn-in, which occurs when there is too much power sent to sub-pixels for a prolonged period, which damages the organic compound. Finally, OLEDs consume a lot of power and generate a lot more heat than their counterparts.

7.4.2 White OLED

To reduce cost, white OLED was introduced more recently (fig. 49).

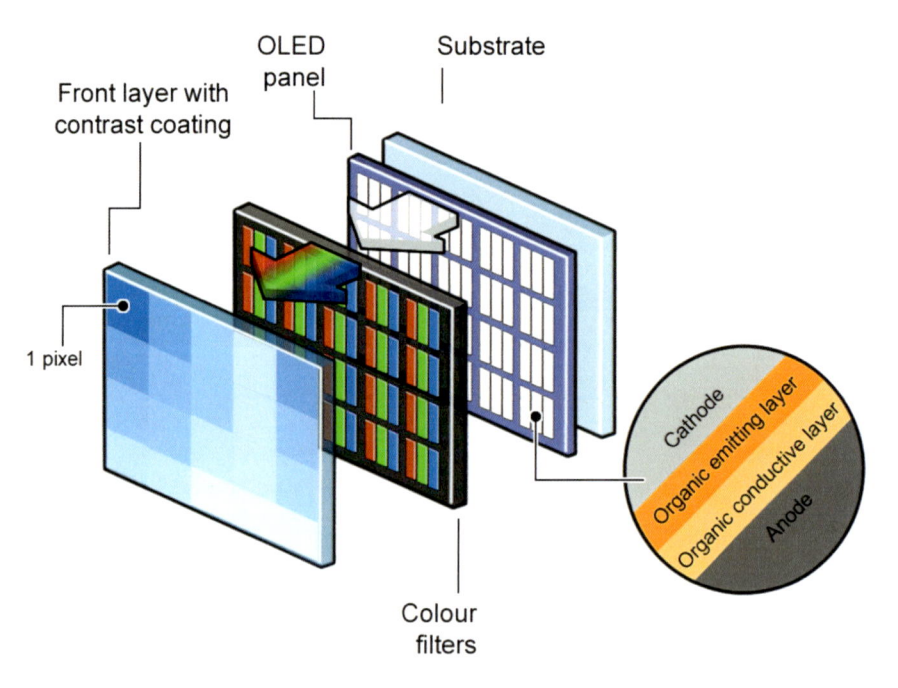

Figure 49 - White OLED display. Source:
https://www.flatpanelshd.com/focus.php?subaction=showfull&id=1474618766

In a nutshell, white OLED is an OLED panel without the RGB subpixels, using color filters instead to generate the color gamut. While it maintains the incredible, additive contrast of RGB OLED, it costs significantly less to manufacture. This comes at the cost of color integrity, though, as it has a narrower gamut than RGB OLED.

7.4.3 QD-OLED

The latest newcomer in the OLED family is Quantum Dot OLED. Similarly to QLED, QD-OLED starts with blue OLED, then goes through an enhancement layer to generate red and green (fig. 50).

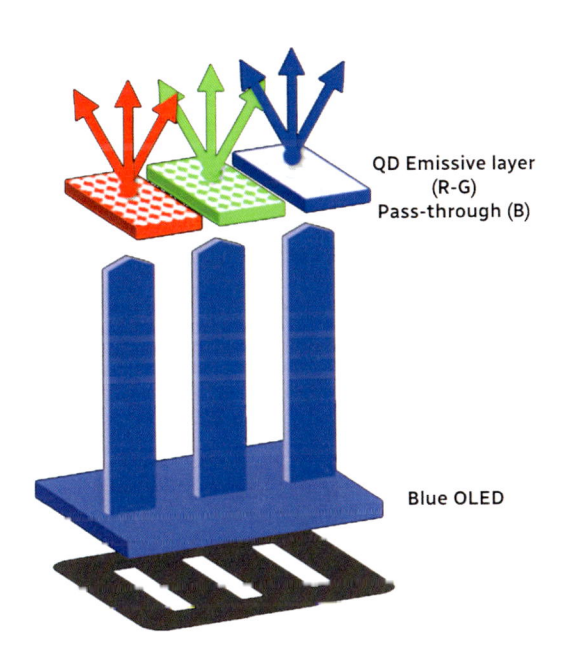

Figure 50 - QD-OLED display. Source:
https://flandersscientific.com/img/WOLED-QDOLED-EmissionType.PNG

This allows QD-OLED to provide a wider color gamut than white OLED, while also retaining its fully emissive properties for light intensity.

7.5 MicroLED

The last family of display technologies we will cover in this guide is MicroLED. As the name implies, these panels are made of tiny light-emitting diodes. They are arranged in arrays of red, green, and blue sub-pixels (fig. 51). Typically, a thin-film transistor is rapidly powering the different sub-pixels and the refresh rate is very high due to the rapid fall time of LEDs, or, in other words, their capacity to get back to full dark after being powered.

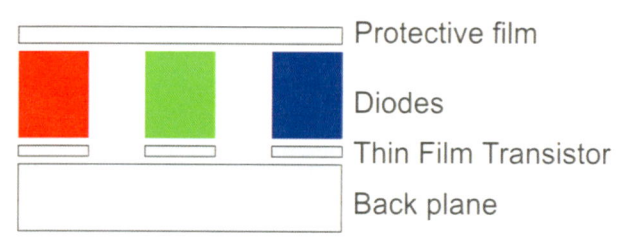

Figure 51 – A MicroLED pixel

In MicroLEDs, light intensity is additive, providing them with very high contrast and complete blacks like OLEDs. Since diodes are inorganic, they do not suffer from burn-in and rapid wear. As the light-emitting diodes are located right behind a thin protective film, they offer a very high angle of viewing without noticeable color skewing, making them ideal for certain applications like digital signage and virtual backgrounds for film and TV production.

The major downsides of MicroLED have to do with the complexity of the fabrication and assembly processes, which drive cost significantly upwards and the relative novelty of the technology, another important cost driver.

When large implementations are required, MicroLED panels are stitched together (fig. 52). This enables rapid maintenance and repair and keeps the panel size relatively small for manufacturing and transport.

Figure 52 – A MicroLED tile – part of a large screen array

When MicroLEDs are used in front of the cameras, there are several production considerations that the practitioner should be aware of. First, it may be challenging to reach panel uniformity through the lens. If we recall, a camera's spectral sensitivity is not matched perfectly to the human eye, and it won't necessarily be matched to the MicroLED panel either, which means that the array may look uniform to the eye and not to the camera, and vice-versa.

Additionally, when the MicroLED array of panels is in focus, the pattern of the subpixels may interfere with the Bayer pattern in Single Large Sensors, creating a *Moiré* effect, similar to aliasing artifacts, which will vary depending on distance and can be very noticeable (fig. 53).

Figure 53 – Moiré effect on a MicroLED panel when shot through a SLS camera.

This phenomenon is typically reduced by using smaller pitch, effectively reducing the black gaps between subpixels and from pixel to pixel, or by using diffusion filters in front of the screen, or an anti-aliasing filter in the camera (although this will also reduce the overall detail level).

7.6 Typical uses - different display technologies

The list below is indicative of the typical use one could make of the different display technologies mentioned above:

7.6.1 LCD
LCD is an older technology providing low-cost screens with decent peak brightness but low contrast in the darks. As such, it is well suited for low-cost flat screen displays in the home, and when screen size is an important factor.

A more recent development is to use a dual LCD panel to reduce crosstalk and thus, increase performance in the dark areas of the image. Sony is one of the companies using this technology in its professional monitors instead of OLED.

7.6.2 OLED
OLED has decent peak brightness, but risks burn-in on stills and high intensity content. It has outstanding contrast in the darks and a wide color gamut. It is relatively expensive and limited in screen size. Given its relative fragility but outstanding low light performance, it is well suited for high-end home theater setups with lighting control as well as for reference monitors.

7.6.3 QLED
QLED has high peak brightness, and decent contrast in the darks. It is less expensive than OLED and allows for larger screen sizes. It is well suited for the home and environments where lighting is less well controlled.

7.6.4 Micro LED
MicroLED is quite expensive and relatively fragile. It requires skilled technical support to setup and install the tiles required. It has high peak brightness and great contrast in the darks. Due to those constraints and characteristics, it is well suited for commercial large applications, like signage and on-set background screens, especially given their very wide angle of viewing.

IN CONCLUSION

In this book, we have tried to cover as much as possible to get you started in film and broadcast engineering related positions. Throughout the book, footnotes will steer you towards additional resources if you should need or just desire to dig deeper in some of the technologies mentioned.

You will also find, in the following pages, a glossary of terms used in this document. It should come in handy when acronyms and terms come flying your way, as it so often happens in this industry.

Thank you again for reading this book, and we wish you a successful career in this fascinating and unique field of engineering!

Cheers,

Pierre (Pete) Routhier, Eng., M.Eng.
pierre.routhier@digitaltroublemaker.com
@digitaltroublemaker

GLOSSARY

2K

The initial resolution of the DCI theatrical digital image container, at 2048 x 1080 pixels. Note that the final image displayed is cropped from that container, either at 1998 x 1080 (2K flat) or 2048 x 858 (2K scope).

3-Chip, Charged-Couple Device (3-CCD)

A camera sensor using three individual sensors to capture red, green, and blue colors. Incoming light is split into the three primary colors using prisms.

3:2 pulldown

A method to combine image fields to convert 24 frames per second material to 29.97 fps or 59.94 fields per second.

4:2:0

Color sub-sampling method where the image is split into 4 x 2 pixel arrays; the first digit (4) means all pixels are containing luminance information, the second digit (2) means two pixels from the first row are used for color, and the third digit (0) means no pixels from the second row are used for color.

4:2:2

Color sub-sampling method where the image is split into 4 x 2 pixel arrays; the first digit (4) means all pixels are containing luminance information, the second digit (2) means two pixels from the first row are used for color, and the third digit (2) means two pixels from the second row are used for color.

4:4:4

Color sub-sampling method where the image is split into 4 x 2 pixel arrays; the first digit (4) means all pixels are containing luminance information, the second digit (4) means all four pixels from the first row are used for color, and the third digit (4) means all pixels from the second row are also used for color.

The 4:4:4:4 variant is used to express a full resolution image (4:4:4) with the addition of a full resolution alpha layer, in order to manage image transparency.

4K

Higher digital theatrical resolution, equivalent to 4 times 2K, with a container of 4096 x 2160 pixels. Not to be confused with Ultra-High Definition (see *UHD*).

Aliasing

Visible *artifacts* in an image caused by an insufficient sampling frequency.

Alpha Matting

A method used to manage transparency in a *raster* image, by assigning each pixel of the image with a transparency value. These values are stored in an *alpha* channel, corresponding to the R, G and B channels of the image. Using this information allows a compositing software to overlay the image over other image(s) with the proper degree of transparency.

Alternating fields

A method for presenting a sequence of images on a Cathode Ray Tube television, by alternating temporally sequential images, but reducing their vertical resolution by using only odd, then even lines on the screen. It was developed to reduce bandwidth and reduce flickering on screen.

Analog to Digital Converter (ADC or AD Converter)

A device that converts continuous, analog signals to discrete, digital values. The precision of the AD converter depends on its *bit depth*, i.e. how many discrete code values are used to approximate the analog signal, as well as its sample frequency.

Aperture

The ratio at which the iris on a camera is open.

Artifact

In the context of video, an artifact is a visible degradation of the image, which can be manifested in a single frame or a sequence. Artifacts can be caused by *aliasing*, ADC glitches, *CODEC* issues, etc.

Aspect Ratio (AR)

The ratio of image width to height. SD television had an aspect ratio of 4:3, or 1.33, meaning the width of the image was 1.33 wider than the height. *HDTV* and *UHDTV* have an aspect ratio of 16:9. Social Media has several aspect ratios, from 1:1 (square) to 9:16 (vertical)

Asynchronous

See *probabilistic*.

Automatic Repeat reQuest (ARQ)

In *probabilistic* video, an error control and packet recovery method for data transmission in which the receiver sends an alert to the sender if a packet is missing, so that the sender can resend the missing packet.

B Frame

In *GOP* encoding, a Bi-directional predictive frame.

Banding

A visible *artifact* caused by insufficient code values to describe a gradient in the image.

Bayer pattern

In single-chip cameras, a pattern that is used to capture R, G and B information. The *Bayer* pattern uses a 2x2 pattern with 2 green, 1 red and 1 blue pixels in checkerboard configuration.

Bit Depth

The number of *Code Values* used to *quantize* an analog source in the digital domain, expressed as a base 2 exponent. For example, 8-bit means 2 to the power of 8, or 256 CVs.

BT.2020

Broadcasting service, Television, recommendation number 2020. Describes a wider *color gamut* than BT.709, based on RGB primaries of laser. Often used in HDR.

BT.2035

Broadcasting service, Television, recommendation number 2035: *A reference viewing environment for evaluation of HDTV program material or completed programmes.*

BT.2100

Broadcasting service, Television, recommendation number 2100: *Image parameter values for high dynamic range television for use in production and international programme exchange.* Comprises the BT.2020 color gamut and either the PQ or HLG transfer function for HDR.

BT.709

Broadcasting service, Television, recommendation number 709: *Parameter values for the HDTV standards for production and international programme exchange.* The color gamut of BT.709 is based on CRT phosphor properties and its transfer function is Gamma.

Cathode-Ray Tube (CRT)

Analog television used the CRT technology, which consists of a vacuum tube containing an electron gun which, when fed with a signal, emits an electron beam to display images on a phosphorescent screen in a line-by-line pattern.

Cd/m^2

Candela per meter squared. See *nits*.

Chroma Sub-sampling

A method to reduce the size of video by reducing the number of colors in pixel representation, by a factor of 2 (see 4:2:2) or 4 (see 4:2:0), while maintaining luminance information for each pixel.

Chromakeying

Technique for background removal that uses a specified color as a *key* and assigns transparency to pixels of said color, which enables the compositing of a replacement background. It is widely used for virtual sets, weather, and motion pictures to this day, but getting gradually replaced by other methods of keying like depth mapping.

CIE 1931

Commission Internationale de l'Éclairage, 1931 model. A model that represents the limits of human perception of color in a 2-dimensional model (x, y).

Clipping

An *artifact* generated during capture when a sensor is full and therefore all detail is lost. Comparable to over-exposure in the film world.

CMOS

Complementary, Metal Oxide Semiconductor. The most widely used image sensor technology for digital cameras due to its high-speed capability and low power consumption.

Code Value (CV)

The unit of digital *quantization*. See *Bit depth*.

Codec

Short for COMpression and DECode. Algorithms to reduce the size of audio and video files and/or streams.

Color Gamut

The range of colors that can be reproduced by a system.

Color Temperature

The actual color of the illuminant in a scene (e.g. tungsten light bulbs, neon, LED, etc.). This information is provided to the camera to ensure colors look uniform from shot to shot. The temperature (in Kelvin) corresponds to the measured color of a blackbody radiator (Planck radiator) at said temperature.

Color Volume

The combination of *color gamut* and light intensity that can be reproduced by a system. In a nutshell, all the colors that the system can display from the darkest to the brightest.

Cones

Color receptors in the eye. Mostly concentrated in a small active vision area called the *macula*.

Container

In video, refers to the single file that contains the required assets to view a video file: image, audio, *metadata*, close caption, etc. Example of container formats: Apple Quicktime, Material eXchange Format (MXF) and MatrioshKa Video (MKV).

Dark Fiber

Refers to a dedicated optical fiber for exclusive use by a client. Can comprise the entire optical fiber or a specific range of wavelengths.

Dark noise

Dark noise is a visible artifact in a video capture when the light intensity is so low that it competes with noise in the sensor, making that noise visible in the image. That noise is generated by several sources, including cosmic radiation, heat, and other sources of electromagnetic radiation. It is the digital equivalent of *under exposure* in film.

DCI P3

The color gamut of conventional digital cinema, as defined by the Digital Cinema Initiatives (DCI) consortium.

Debayering

The process of interpolating pixels in a *Bayer pattern* sensor to recreate a full Red, Green, and Blue image.

Depth Of Field (DOF)
The range of depth from the camera point of view where people and objects will appear to be in focus.

Deterministic
By opposition to *Probabilistic*, refers to a transmission protocol where information flows at a pre-determined, predictable pace with ordered frames. *SDI* and *HDMI* are examples of deterministic video transmission.

Director of Photography (DP or DoP)
The person in charge of creative and technical aspects of the image during a production, including lighting, camera and lens selection, image capture parameters and creative look in production and post-production.

Display-referred
An image that is formatted to be presented in a predetermined format to accommodate a display standard like *BT.709*, for example.

Dynamic Range
In video, refers to the range of luminance that can be encoded and displayed. Traditionally expressed as a ratio for displays (e.g. 1000:1), or a base 2 logarithm for capture (e.g. 10 stops – 2^{10} = 4096 to 1)

Electroluminescent
Matter that emits light when submitted to an electrical current.

Electron

Electrical charge unit. In video capture, incoming *photons* hit a sensor, displacing electrons, and thus creating current. By measuring this current, source light intensity can be quantified.

Electro-Optical Transfer Function (EOTF)

The mathematical function used to convert code values to on-display luminance.

Emissive

Emissive display technologies create light intensity and color instantaneously instead of filtering them out from a white back light, which typically provides superior contrast and colors. *OLED* is an example of an emissive technology in displays.

Essence

In a *package*, essences are source components of a complete video file or stream. Typically, a stream will contain a video essence and multiple audio essences.

False Color

A visualization tool to see exposure levels in an image. Exposure level is typically split in color bands graduated from red (over-exposure) to orange, yellow, gray, green, blue, and purple (under-exposure) and overlaid on a grayscale rendition of the image.

Fields per second

In *interlaced* video, the number of alternating fields presented on the display in a second. *NTSC* provisions for 59.94 fields per second, where *PAL* provisions for 50.

File-based video

A pre-recorded video package contained in a computer readable file. By opposition to a *video stream*.

Focal Length

The focal length of a lens is the distance, in millimeters, between the optical center of a lens and the attached camera's sensor when the lens is focused at infinity. Very short focal lengths extend a shot's perspective beyond human vision, making background objects appear very far. Conversely, long focal lengths compress a shot's perspective, making background objects appear closer than they are.

Focus

The focus distance is the distance between a camera's nodal point and where features need to be in front of the camera to appear clearly on the sensor.

Forward Error Correction (FEC)

An error-proofing mechanism used in *probabilistic* video transmission. The principle behind FEC is that the system, when it pushes packets, duplicates some the payload across the network, reducing the risk of packet loss.

Frames per second

Video temporal resolution, in *progressive* formats.

Gamma

The *SD* and *HD transfer function*, which originated in analog *CRT* television. In *High Dynamic Range*, it is replaced by transfer functions *HLG* and *PQ*.

Group-Of-Pictures (GOP)

In *inter-frame* compressed video, a GOP is a cogent unit comprised of *I, P and B frames*, requiring less space to compress than using *inter-frame* compressed video.

Heat Map

see *False Color*

High-Definition Television (HDTV)

The current standard for television, HDTV comes in two formats: 720p, which is 1280x720 progressive frames and 1080i, which is 1920x1080 interlaced fields

High Dynamic Range (HDR)

In video, refers to a wider dynamic range than conventional HDTV. Usually used together with a Wider Color Gamut such as defined in ITU-R BT.2100. HDR can be used in both High-Definition and Ultra-High Definition spatial and temporal resolutions.

High Frame Rate (HFR)

In video, refers to formats with higher frame rate than conventional HDTV, namely 100 fps and 120 fps.

Histogram

In video, visual representation of image luminance, with luminance code values as the x axis and percentage of pixels at each code value on the y axis.

Hybrid Log Gamma (HLG)
One of the two standardized HDR transfer functions in *BT.2100*.

HTTP Live Streaming (HLS)
A *probabilistic* streaming protocol developed by Apple. Mainly used for video streaming.

I frame

In a *GOP*, an *intra-compression* frame. See *Intra Frame*.

ICtCp

A color representation model for *HDR*, standardized in *BT.2100*.

Illuminant

The *color temperature* defined as white on a display system. *HDTV* and *HDR* use D65 as their illuminant, while Digital Cinema uses D60.

InfraRed (IR) pollution and filtering

IR pollution occurs when electromagnetic radiation that is in the invisible IR range of wavelength displaces electrons on a sensor, thus skewing color perception in the captured image. Countered by using IR filters, either built in the camera or external.

Inter-frame

In video, frame compression that is dependent on other frames within a *Group-Of-Pictures*. While it is more size efficient than *Intra-frame* compression, it requires buffering as the whole GOP needs to be in memory to reconstruct the frame sequence.

Interlaced

See *Alternating Fields*.

Intra-frame

Intra-frame compression. In video, refers to frames which do not have any inter-dependency with other frames in a video sequence, and can therefore be decoded by themselves without any buffering.

Judder

A perceptible motion artifact affecting perceived motion fluidity. Typically occurs when inconsistent frame rates and shutter speeds are used.

Keying

Assigning a level of transparency to pixels in an image based on color (see *chromakeying*), luminance, depth, or other methods, to compose the image with another (typically replacing the image's background).

Latency

The time interval between the creation of a video frame and its delivery on the display.

Latitude

The dynamic *range* of a capture system. Expressed in "stops", which are a base 2 exponent. For example, a camera with a latitude of 10 stops has a dynamic range of 2^{10} or 4096:1

Letterbox

Using black lines above and below an image with a high aspect ratio to make it fit within a frame with a lower aspect ratio. Typically used to make cinema frames (1.85:1 or 2.35:1) fit inside video's 1.78:1 AR.

Light Emitting Diode (LED)

Diodes emitting light when under current. Used to generate the backlight of a classic LCD display.

Liquid Crystal Display (LCD)

Display using the polarizing characteristics of liquid crystal to filter light out, thus creating contrast.

Luminance

The brightness of a display, measured in *nits*.

Macula

The region in the eye responsible for color perception and fine vision.

Magnification

Increasing the size of an image without changing its perspective.

Megapixel

One million pixels.

Metadata

In video, information which is not audio or video but rather string or text based, like date of creation, sub-titles, color volume identification, etc.

Mezzanine

A high bitrate file format rendered from post-production to provide a high-quality archival asset. Used by distribution to transcode all distribution formats and bitrates more efficiently than re-rendering the source assets every time.

Micro LED

Display technology which uses very small Light Emitting Diodes as direct illumination. Each pixel consists of a Red, Green, and Blue subpixel.

Motion Blur

Blurriness in an image due to relative motion in the frame during exposure.

MPEG-DASH

Stands for *MPEG, Dynamic Adaptive Streaming over HTTP*. An open streaming protocol for streaming content over the existing HTTP infrastructure. Competitor to Apple's HLS.

National Television Systems Committee (NTSC)

North American committee that created the standard for digital *Standard Definition* television in North America.

Network Time Protocol (NTP)

A protocol to set time on network connected devices like smartphones, tablets, and computers.

Nits

Unit of emissive luminance for displays. In the metric system, 1 nit equals to 1 candela per meter squared, or *cd/m^2*.

OETF

Opto-Electrical (or electronic) Transfer Function. A mathematical representation of how incoming luminance information converts to code values in the digital realm.

OOTF

Opto-Optical Transfer Function. The overall "glass to glass" transfer of luminance from what is measured in front of a camera to how it translates to luminance on a display. It is a combination of *OETF* and *EOTF*.

OpenEXR

An image format which contains enough CVs to encompass the entire human visual system in terms of color and dynamic range perception. Used by the Academy of Motion Pictures Arts and Science for their open-source ACES format.

Organic, Light Emitting Diode (OLED)

A display technology using the electroluminescent properties of its organic compound to generate light. OLED displays are *emissive* in nature, providing high contrast with deep blacks.

Outside Broadcast (OB)

Refers to a remote production that is located outside a broadcast center, typically in an OB truck or van at a given venue (e.g. sports arena).

Over-The-Top (OTT)

An on-demand, streaming service on the internet. By opposition to traditional linear broadcast.

P frame

In a *Group Of Pictures*, refers to a predictive frame.

Packaging

In video, refers to a solution that integrates audio and video *essences* as well as *metadata* in a single file or stream.

Packet

In *Predictive* video streaming, a packet is the smallest chunk of information sent through the network.

Phase Alternating Line (PAL)

The *Standard Definition* TV format outside of North America.

Photon

The energy particle of light.

Pillarbox

Using black lines to the left and the right of an image with a low aspect ratio to make it fit within a frame with a higher aspect ratio. Typically used to fit vertical video (9:16) inside a HD frame (16:9) or *SD* inside *HD*.

Pixel

The basic unit of image resolution. Each pixel normally contains three sub-pixels (on displays) or channels (in a file or stream) for R, G and B information.

PIZ

A lossless compression format used in OpenEXR to reduce file size.

Portable Network Graphics (PNG)

An image format which also contains an *alpha channel*. Typically used for stills, in *raster*-based graphics.

PQ

Perceptual Quantizer. A transfer function developed by Dolby laboratories to quantize luminance in relationship to human perception of changes in shade. Standardized under ST.2084 for *High Dynamic Range* video.

Precision Time Protocol (PTP)

A timing protocol developed for synchronization of computers in a network. Used in ST.2110 *predictive*, Internet Protocol transmission of video. Standardized as IEEE 1588.

Prime Lens

A camera lens with a fixed *focal length*, by opposition to a *zoom* lens.

Probabilistic

In video, refers to breaking down source video into packets, which are sent through a network to a destination, where packets are re-aligned temporally to reconstruct the stream for visualization. As packets travel through different paths in the network, some *latency* is required to provide sufficient time for all packets to reach their destination. May include error correction mechanisms like *FEC* to mitigate lost or late packets.

Progressive

Progressive video formats present a full frame simultaneously, as opposed to time-shifted *interlaced* and *psf* formats.

Progressive, Segmented Frames (psf)

A technique to encode progressive frames in an interlaced system. The progressive frame is broken down in odd and even lines then sent through the interlaced system. A flag indicates to the destination that the source is progressive, and the system will buffer both odd and even fields to present a full progressive frame to the display.

QD Oled

A display technology using a *Quantum Dot* enhancement layer in combination with blue *OLED* to create RGB light. Provides wider color gamut than *White OLED*.

Quality of Service (QoS)

In video, refers to the metrics used to quantify the reliability of a video service to deliver. Can also refer to the underlying technologies used to mitigate reliability issues caused by packet loss, delays, and data corruption in the network.

Quantizing

Assigning discrete, digital *Code Values* to ranges of continuous values from an analog signal. Insufficient CVs in quantizing can potentially lead to *banding artifacts*, whereas too many CVs lead to higher *bitrates* and unnecessarily large file or stream sizes, requiring additional memory and computing power.

Quantum Efficiency (QE)

In a sensor, QE refers to the percentage of conversion from photons to electrons.

Quantum-dot Light Emitting Diode, Liquid Crystal Display (QLED LCD)

A display technology using blue *LED* and a *QD* enhancement layer to generate a narrower wavelength white backlight, resulting in wider color gamut images than traditional *LCD* displays.

R, G, B

Red, Green, and Blue colors, corresponding to the sensitivity of human *cones*, and consequently used in display technologies to emulate real-world colors.

Raster Graphics

Graphics based on a pixel array. Requires larger file sizes and less scalable than *vector* graphics but allows photorealism.

Real-Time Messaging Protocol (RTMP)

A low latency open-source streaming protocol for audio, video and metadata developed by Adobe.

Real-time Timing Protocol (RTP)

A streaming protocol for delivering audio and video over IP networks

RGB Oled

an *OLED* display technology where each pixel is comprised of an *emissive* Red, Green, and Blue subpixel.

Rods

In the human eye, rods convey luminance as well as motion information to the brain through the optic nerve.

S, M, L

The range of wavelengths that the human eye can perceive. S (which stands for Small) is equivalent to 420 nanometers (perceived as blue), M (medium) to 534nm (green) and L (large) to 564 nm (red).

Scene-linear

Refers to an image in which the luminance is encoded in a linear fashion, in direct relationship to the source in front of the camera, independently of display technologies and formats. Typically used in camera raw formats.

Scene-referred

Refers to an image in which the luminance is encoded in a non-linear fashion (e.g. logarithmic), in direct relationship to the source in front of the camera, independently of display technologies and formats. An example of a scene-referred format is ArriRAW, Arri's proprietary 12-bit logarithmic (LogC) format.

Secure, Reliable Transport (SRT)

A streaming protocol developed by Haivision.

Serial Digital Interface (SDI)

A *deterministic* video transport protocol used in broadcasting.

Spatial Resolution

The number of pixels (width x length) in the raster scan of an image.

ST.2084

See Perceptual Quantizer (PQ).

ST.2110

A standard for high quality streaming of media over managed IP networks.

Standard Definition TV

The initial format for digital television, with a lower resolution than HDTV. See:

https://simple.wikipedia.org/wiki/Standard-definition_television

Super Hi Vision

A super high resolution video format at 7680 x 4320, or four times UHD TV

Synchronous

See *Deterministic*.

Tag Image File Format (TIFF)

An image format which can also contain an *alpha channel*. Typically used for stills, in *raster*-based graphics, as well as image sequences.

Telephoto Lens

A *prime* lens with a high focal length. Compresses the perspective as compared to human vision.

Temporal Resolution

The number of frames per second in a video.

Thin Film Transistor (TFT)

In *LCD* displays, the TFT allows rapid addressing of the LCD matrix to achieve high frame rates.

Transfer Function

In video, refers to the mathematical model used to represent the relationship between luminance and code values.

Tri-stimulus model

The graphic representation of human vision using Red, Green, and Blue primaries.

Ultra HD

A very high-resolution format with 4 times the HD resolution at 3840 pixels wide by 2160 pixels high.

Vector Graphics

Graphics generated on the spot with coded vectorial instructions. Much smaller in size than *raster graphics* but limited in photorealism.

Vectorscope

Monitoring tool to objectively measure color hue and saturation.

Waveform Monitor

Monitoring tool to objectively measure luminance distribution across an image, from left to right.

Web-based, Real Time Communication (WebRTC)

A low latency video streaming protocol.

Wide Area Network (WAN)

A telecommunications network that extends over a large geographic area. Not necessarily connected to the internet.

White Balance

Adjusting a camera's RGB levels to ensure white integrity based on the scene's *illuminant*.

White OLED

A display technology using white OLED to add light intensity and color filters at the sub-pixel level to subtract colors.

x, y, Y

A tri-dimensional model to represent *color volume* in video.

YCbCr

A model for color representation in digital video.

YUV

A model for color representation in uncompressed digital and analog video.

Zoom

A variable focal length lens assembly.

Printed in the USA
CPSIA information can be obtained
at www.ICGtesting.com
LVRC092137160624
783073LV00049B/64